THE WAY
CAMINO
CAMINHO

EDUARDO
CALDERAN
QUINTINO

editora
caminho

2025

AOS QUE EXISTIRAM PARA
QUE EU PUDESSE SER

A QUIENES ME ANTECEDIERON
PARA QUE YO PUDIERA EXISTIR

FOR THOSE WHO CAME FIRST,
SO THAT I COULD BE

Joe
Sofie
k Téged!
Jézus

CRn2
CRn2

De 13'00h a 15'00h y de 18'00h a 21'00h

quechua

IN STYLE

LA CIVILIZACION ESTA EN CRISIS
¡¡¡OREMOS
DIVINO

KOKS
FRANS
BELGIE

Fly Emirates
9

CAMINO DE SANTIAGO
LORCA (Navarra)
CIRAUQUI

CAMINO
DE
SANTIAGO
ITINERARIO
CULTURAL EUROPEO
DE EUROPA

EU CEDO

Na penumbra, protagonizo o vagaroso ritual de deixar a cama, cuidar do corpo, fechar a mochila. E partir, no tempo exato em que a madrugada começa a ceder ao dia. Atravessa o som dos meus próprios passos a peculiar sensação de pertencimento. No ajuste fino entre a prontidão do corpo, da mente e da alma e o despertar de toda vida ao meu redor, testemunho a magia da sincronicidade com o ciclo circadiano.

O dia me apresenta sombras longas. Entretido com sua variável imensidão, me pego brincando com essas projeções do corpo que ultrapassam montanhas e a consciência em expansão. Essas elevações contam sobre o vento e a quietude. Enquanto construo um silêncio interno desafiador, convivo com minha tentativa sofrida de me apropriar dele.

Fico à flor da pele, como pedra sem reboco, manifesta na passagem.

Meu bicho-homem avança, desentocando hábitos e sensações que correm soltas dentro de mim, sempre vulnerável e acessível ao acaso. O Caminho sugere camaradagem. Ajudar e aceitar ajuda. Interdependência. Dou boas-vindas a trocas breves e profundas.

O contínuo e repetitivo esforço físico me conta mais sobre como lidar com dores e variações de humor. Participo da esperada demanda por alimentos, enquanto o oco das caramanholas vazias proclama desgaste e sede. Sou premiado pela curiosidade gastronômica que ultrapassa barreiras.

Opero, com meus botões, a força multitarefa que administra equipamentos, pessoas, situações inesperadas e incessantes, além das subpersonalidades.

Encontro os mais velhos do Caminho e me entrego ao tempo dilatado. Ali permaneço e aprendo sobre o recolhimento e a solidão, mas também sobre solitude e companheirismo. Às vezes, o alto astral permeia a conversa com esses aposentados que parecem estar sempre à disposição de quem passa.

Digo o mundo fotografando. O retratado e eu, o retratista e os registros, lado a lado, a par e passo, atentos ao diálogo justo das entrelinhas do ofício.

Percebo como a qualidade do humor de cada hospitaleiro impacta o ânimo do peregrino e como a recíproca é também verdadeira. Sou mais um passante-transformador. Trago novidades, não permaneço e, desde logo, me desencaixo do lugar.

Dia a dia, tenho ponto de partida e de chegada. Sucessão de paradas num ritmo de tempos singulares.

Peregrino, eu me entrego a um propósito, ainda que jamais saiba qual seja.

YO CEDO

Me levanto temprano y protagonizo el sereno ritual matutino de salir de la cama, cuidar del cuerpo, cerrar la mochila, echar a andar y ver cómo la noche se transforma en día. Al compás de mis propios pasos, llevo conmigo la peculiar sensación de sentirme integrado. En el ajuste fino entre la prontitud de cuerpo, mente y alma y el despertar de todo y de todos, soy testigo de la magia de la sincronicidad con el ciclo circadiano.

El día me presenta sombras alargadas, me entretengo con su variable inmensidad y me pillo jugueteando con esas proyecciones del cuerpo que cruzan montañas, la consciencia en expansión. Las montañas hablan sobre el viento y la quietud. Construyo un silencio interno desafiante, convivo con el intento sufrido de apropiarme de él.

Estoy a flor de piel, como piedra sin enlucir, expuesta al medio.

Mi yo animal avanza despertando hábitos y sensaciones escondidas que afloran dentro de mí, siempre vulnerable y abierto al azar. El Camino sugiere compañerismo. Ayudar y ser ayudado. Interdependencia. Valoro los intercambios breves y profundos.

El esfuerzo físico continuo y repetitivo me enseña a manejar los dolores y cambios de humor. Participo en la esperada demanda de alimentos mientras el sonido a hueco de las cantimploras insuficientes proclama desgaste y sed. Mi curiosidad gastronómica me recompensa al superar barreras

Trabajo internamente el esfuerzo multitarea que implica el manejo de equipos, personas, situaciones inesperadas e incesantes y, por supuesto, mis subpersonalidades.

Encuentro a los más mayores del Camino y me entrego a un tiempo dilatado. Permanezco y aprendo sobre aislamiento y soledad, pero también sobre introspección y compañerismo. A veces, el buen humor impregna la conversación con estos jubilados a disposición de quien pase.

Expreso el mundo fotografiando. El retratado y yo, el retratista y los registros, lado a lado, paso a paso, atentos al diálogo justo de las entrelíneas del oficio.

Percibo cómo el humor de cada hospitalero en el Camino impacta en el ánimo del peregrino y viceversa. Soy otro caminante transformador. Traigo novedades, no permanezco y, sin duda, no encajo en el lugar.

Día a día tengo un punto de partida y otro de llegada.
Una sucesión de paradas a un ritmo singular.

Como peregrino, tengo un propósito, aunque jamás sepa cuál es.

I SURRENDER

Early in the morning, I perform the slow ritual of getting out of bed, taking care of my body, and zipping the backpack to watch the night turn into a new day. The peculiar feeling of belonging crosses the sounds of my own footsteps. In the fine tuning between the promptitude of the body, mind and soul, and the awakening of everything and everyone, I witness the magical synchronicity with the circadian cycle.

The day displays long shadows. I am absorbed by its fluid immensity and find myself toying with shapes projected by my body that go beyond mountains and expanded consciousness. Those rises talk about wind and stillness. Building up a defiant inner silence, I live with my painful attempt to embody it.

I feel sensitive, raw, a wall without plaster, a stone manifested along the way.

The animal in myself advances, flushing out habits and sensations that run rampant inside, as I am always vulnerable and open to chance. The Camino inspires fellowship. It is about helping and accepting help. Interdependence. I welcome transient and profound exchanges.

The uninterrupted and repetitive physical exertion tells me further how to deal with pain and mood swings. I participate in the expected demand for food, while the void of scarce water bottles announces fatigue and thirst. I am awarded with a gastronomic curiosity that overcomes barriers.

I deal alone with the multitasking ability to manage equipment, people, unexpected and unceasing situations, and even my sub-personalities.

By meeting the elders of the Camino, I surrender to the expanded time. I stay and learn about withdrawal and loneliness, but also about solitude and companionship. Sometimes high spirits pervade the conversation with these retirees available to passersby.

I proclaim the world by photographing. What is reproduced and myself, the photographer and the records, side by side, step by step, attentive to the fair dialogue between the lines of this craft.

I realize how the mood of every single host affects the animus of each pilgrim; the other way around is also true. I am just another transformer passerby. I bring news, I don't stay and, right away, I no longer take part.

Day after day, I have a starting and an ending point. A succession of stops in a bar of peculiar rhythms.

As a pilgrim, I devote myself to a purpose, even if I never know what it is.

OCEANO AT
SANTIAGO DE COMPOSTELA
FINISTERRA
ARZÚA
MELIDE
VENTAS DE NARÓN
SAMOS
O CEBREIRO
TRABADELO
COLUMBRIANOS
EL ACEBO DE SAN MIGUEL
MURIAS DE RECHIVALDO
HOSPITAL DE ÓRBIGO
LEÓN
VIRGEN DEL CAMINO
MANSILLA DE LAS MULAS
CALZADILLA DE LOS HERMANILLOS
SAHAGÚN
CALZADI
POBLACIÓN DE CAMPO
VIGO
PORTO
COIMBRA
PORTUGAL
VALLADOLID
SALAMANCA
ES
MA

NTICO
FRANÇA
SAINT-JEAN-PIED-DE-PORT
PAU
LOURDES
ORISSON
ZUBIRI
RONCESVALLES
PAMPLONA
CIRAUQUI
EUNATE
ESTELLA
LOS ARCOS
LOGROÑO
VIANA
NÁJERA
BELORADO
SANTO DOMINGO DE LA CALZADA
URGOS
SAN JUAN DE ORTEGA
DEL CAMINO
HUESCA
ZARAGOZA
A N H A
1ª VIAGEM 27 JUL A 16 AGO 2015
[EDUARDO E AULUS, 500 KM]
2ª VIAGEM 25 SET A 13 OUT 2017
[EDUARDO E CLAUDIA, 300 KM]
PERNOITES
MAR MEDITERRÂNEO

Inserido no retrato
Fróximo a Irache.

Encajado en el paisaje
Cerca de Irache.

Blending with the portrait
Near Irache.

Vi um labirinto de pedra e me aventurei
Próximo a Burgos.

Vi un laberinto de piedra y me aventuré
Cerca de Burgos.

I saw a labyrinth of rocks and embraced a chance
Near Burgos.

Trouxeram pedras
Cruz de Fierro, Foncebadón.

Trajeron piedras
Cruz de Fierro, Foncebadón.

They brought stones
Cruz de Fierro, Foncebadón.

Resiliência e solitude
Próximo a Irache.

Resiliencia y soledad
Cerca de Irache.

Resilience and solitude
Near Irache.

O mesmo vento penteava crinas e cabelos
Pirineus.

El mismo viento peinaba crines y cabellos
Pirineos.

The same wind has combed manes and hair
Pyrenees.

Trajeto antes que a mata feche
Próximo a Ponferrada.

Trayecto antes de que el bosque se cierre
Cerca de Ponferrada.

The path before the forest take it
Near Ponferrada.

Fresta
Na imagem, Claudia Oliva.
Floresta de Navarra.

Intersticio
En la imagen, Claudia Oliva.
Bosque en Navarra.

Aperture
In the picture, Claudia Oliva.
Navarra Forest.

Entre indizível e inexplicável
Meseta, próximo a Léon.

Entre lo indecible y lo inexplicable
Meseta, cerca de León.

Unspeakable / inexplicable – a fine line
Meseta, near León.

Cobiçada imersão do leito da nuvem
Pirineus.

Anhelada inmersión del lecho de la nube
Pirineos.

Coveted plunge in a bed of clouds
Pyrenees.

Eu sou outro. Eu sou o outro
O Cebreiro.

Soy otro. Soy el otro
O Cebreiro.

I am another one. I am the other one
O Cebreiro.

Desjejum com os anjos
Último dia de caminhada, Arzúa.

Desayuno con los ángeles
Último día de caminata, Arzúa.

Breakfast with angels
Last day of hiking, Arzúa.

Esperança na névoa
Próximo a Cruz de Fierro, Foncebadón.

Esperanza en la niebla
Cerca de Cruz de Fierro, Foncebadón.

Hope in the haze
Near Cruz de Fierro, Foncebadón.

Nova pele na Terra
Próximo a Foncebadón.

Nueva piel en la Tierra
Cerca de Foncebadón.

A new skin layer on Earth
Near Foncebadón.

Gigantes
Pirineus.

Gigantes
Pirineos.

Giants
Pyrenees.

Ele se basta
Pirineus.

Él se basta
Pirineos.

By himself is enough
Pyrenees.

Desconcertos d'água
Aulus Sellmer no rio Samos, Sarria.

Desconciertos del agua
Aulus Sellmer en el río Samos, Sarria.

Dis-concert(ing) in waters
Aulus Sellmer at Samos river, Sarria.

As carpas sentem o andor
Próximo a Logroño.

Las carpas sienten la levedad
Cerca de Logroño.

Carps on the processional litter
Near Logroño.

Nada detém sonhar
Próximo a Rabanal del Camino.

Nada detiene el soñar
Cerca de Rabanal del Camino.

Nothing prevents dreaming
Near Rabanal del Camino.

O passado no devir
Villafranca del Bierzo.

El pasado en el porvenir
Villafranca del Bierzo.

The past in what come to be
Villafranca del Bierzo.

Abandono e memória
Próximo a Ponferrada.

Abandono y recuerdo
Cerca de Ponferrada.

Abandonment and recollection
Near Ponferrada.

Degraus missionários
Pe. Valentín em Roncesvalles.

Escalones misioneros
P. Valentín en Roncesvalles.

Missionary steps
Fr. Valentín in Roncesvalles.

Janelas ao acaso
Roncesvalles.

Ventanas al azar
Roncesvalles.

Windows adrift
Roncesvalles.

A hóstia necessária
Pe. Labiano em Roncesvalles.

La hostia necesaria
P. Labiano en Roncesvalles.

The necessary holy host
Fr. Labiano in Roncesvalles.

Congregação do dever
A Missa do Peregrino, Roncesvalles.

Congregación del deber
La Misa del Peregrino, Roncesvalles.

Congregation of duty
Pilgrim's Mass, Roncesvalles.

Sem tradução
Villamayor de Monjardín.

Sin traducción
Villamayor de Monjardín.

No translation
Villamayor de Monjardín.

Vigília dos justos
Rio Arga.

Vigilia de los justos
Río Arga.

Just the vigil of the just
Arga River.

Em linguagem vegetal
Nossa única peregrinação noturna.
Fim da Meseta, próximo a León.

En lenguaje vegetal
Nuestra única peregrinación nocturna.
Fin de la Meseta, cerca de León.

In the language of plants
Our sole night pilgrimage.
The end of Meseta, near León.

Arfar das pedras
Próximo a Torres del Río.

Jadeo de las piedras
Cerca de Torres del Río.

Gasping stones
Near Torres del Río.

A imanência das amoras
Zubiri.

La inmanencia de las moras
Zubiri.

The immanence of blackberries
Zubiri.

Parceria na relva
Pirineus.

Compañerismo en la pradera
Pirineos.

Befriending on the green carpet
Pyrenees.

Vindima encantada
Ferreiros.

Vendimia encantada
Ferreiros.

Enchanted vintage
Ferreiros.

Olho mágico
Próximo a Ayegui.

Mirilla
Cerca de Ayegui.

Peephole
Near Ayegui.

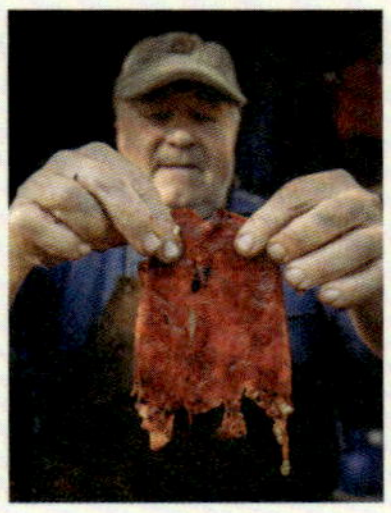

Viver é vermelho
Castildelgado.

Vivir es rojo
Castildelgado.

Living is red
Castildelgado.

No trajeto da quietude
Entre Samos e Sarria.

En el trayecto de la quietud
Entre Samos y Sarria.

On the serenity road
Between Samos and Sarria.

Pausa vertebrada
Cruz de Fierro, Foncebadón.

Pausa vertebrada
Cruz de Fierro, Foncebadón.

A vertebrate pause
Cruz de Fierro, Foncebadón.

Rodas síncronas
Hornillos del Camino,
início da Meseta.

Ruedas acompasadas
Hornillos del Camino,
principio de la Meseta.

Wheels in sync
Hornillos del Camino,
the start of Meseta.

Acaso do sol a pino
Entre O Cebreiro e Samos.

A pleno sol
Entre O Cebreiro y Samos.

The fortune of an overhead sun
Between O Cebreiro and Samos.

Varal de historicidades
Albergue Municipal de O Cebreiro.

Tendedero de historicidades
Albergue Municipal de O Cebreiro.

Lines of historicities
O Cebreiro Municipal Hostel.

Renovar a marcha
Albergue Municipal de O Cebreiro.

Renovar la marcha
Albergue Municipal de O Cebreiro.

Refreshing the pace
O Cebreiro Municipal Hostel.

Matilde indecifrável
Venta Celta, ponto de encontro e alimento. O Cebreiro.

Matilde indescifrable
Venta Celta, punto de encuentro y comida. O Cebreiro.

Non-decodable Matilde
Venta Celta, a meeting and feeding point. O Cebreiro.

Generosidade
Jesús Jato, Villafranca del Bierzo.

Generosidad
Jesús Jato, Villafranca del Bierzo.

Generosity
Jesús Jato, Villafranca del Bierzo.

Concórdia
Templário Tomás Martínez, Manjarín.

Concordia
Templario Tomás Martínez, Manjarín.

Consonance
Templar Tomás Martínez, Manjarín.

Querido e seguido
Arzúa.

Querido y seguido
Arzúa.

Beloved and followed
Arzúa.

Desenraizados de si mesmos
Peregrinos italianos saindo de Ferreiro.

Desarraigados de sí mismos
Peregrinos italianos saliendo de Ferreiro.

Ungrounded from themselves
Italian pilgrims leaving Ferreiro.

Sem medo, sem documento
Entre Pamplona e Puente la Reina.

Sin miedo, sin documento
Entre Pamplona y Puente la Reina.

No fear, no name
Between Pamplona and Puente la Reina.

Além da liberdade
Estella.

Más allá de la liberta
Estella.

Far beyond freedom
Estella.

Comunhão
Estella.

Comunión
Estella.

Communion
Estella.

Ao lado das águas correntes
Saint-Jean-Pied-de-Port.

Al lado de las aguas corrientes
Saint-Jean-Pied-de-Por.

Parallel to running waters
Saint-Jean-Pied-de-Port.

Geometria do Sol
Monastério de Samos.

Geometría del Sol
Monasterio de Samos.

The geometry of the Sun
Monastery of Samos.

Conforto ancorado no céu
Palácio Episcopal de Astorga, obra de Antoni Gaudí.

Confort anclado en el cielo
Palacio Episcopal de Astorga, obra de Antoni Gaudí.

Blessings anchored in the sky
Episcopal Palace of Astorga, Antoni Gaudí's work.

Estrelas guias
Albergue de San Antón, Castrojeriz.

Estrellas guía
Albergue de San Antón, Castrojeriz.

Guiding stars
San Antón Hostel, Castrojeriz.

Na moldura da humanidade
Albergue de San Antón, Castrojeriz.

En el marco de la humanidad
Albergue de San Antón, Castrojeriz.

In the frame of humanity
San Antón Hostel, Castrojeriz.

Vício da forma
Estella.

Adicción a la forma
Estella.

Praxis addiction
Estella.

Em sociedade
Ruínas de San Antón, Castrojeriz.

En sociedad
Ruinas de San Antón, Castrojeriz.

In society
San Antón ruins, Castrojeriz.

A sombra integra o fim e o recomeço
Piso da Plaza do Obradoiro, Santiago de Compostela.

La sombra integra el fin y el recomienzo
Suelo de la Plaza del Obradoiro, Santiago de Compostela.

The shadow coalesces the end and a new beginning
The floor at Plaza del Obradoiro, Santiago de Compostela.

O cheiro da sujeição desejada
Catedral de Santiago de Compostela.

El aroma de la sujeción deseada
Catedral de Santiago de Compostela.

The scent of a desired surrender
Santiago de Compostela Cathedral.

Praça da celebração
Plaza do Obradoiro, Santiago de Compostela.

Plaza de la celebración
Plaza del Obradoiro, Santiago de Compostela.

Celebration square
Plaza del Obradoiro, Santiago de Compostela.

Sentimentos se transpassam
Plaza do Obradoiro, Santiago de Compostela.

Sentimientos se traspasan
Plaza del Obradoiro, Santiago de Compostela.

Crisscrossed feelings
Plaza del Obradoiro, Santiago de Compostela.

O enigma do instante
Praça do Obradoiro, Santiago de Compostela.

El enigma del instante
Plaza del Obradoiro, Santiago de Compostela.

The riddle of an instant
Plaza del Obradoiro, Santiago de Compostela.

Lembrança e esquecimento
Plaza do Obradoiro, Santiago de Compostela.

Recuerdo y olvido
Plaza del Obradoiro, Santiago de Compostela.

Remembrance and oblivion
Plaza del Obradoiro, Santiago de Compostela.

O BICIGRINO E O PEREGRINO (2015)

Recebi o convite de Aulus Sellmer, reconhecido preparador físico e um dos idealizadores do projeto "Desafios pelo Mundo", para documentar sua peregrinação pelo Caminho de Santiago, em 2015.
Durante a jornada, ele enviava boletins diários para as rádios Eldorado e Estadão, de São Paulo, narrando suas experiências ao longo do percurso. Por questões de logística, para carregar os equipamentos fotográficos necessários, optei pela bicicleta. Ele seguiu a pé.
E assim nos tornamos uma dupla incomum: eu, bicigrino; ele, peregrino.
Ele partiu de Saint-Jean-Pied-de-Port, início do Caminho Francês. Eu só fui encontrá-lo 300 km adiante, em Burgos, para seguirmos juntos dali até Santiago de Compostela, percorrendo 500 km em 21 dias.
Logo que nos encontramos, Aulus compartilhou comigo suas vivências pelo Caminho — histórias, símbolos e tudo aquilo que os passos haviam lhe ensinado.
A liberação de qualquer peso extra foi o mote da jornada que criou, desde o início, uma constante: a reorganização de equipamentos, acessórios e objetos pessoais; os consequentes despachos libertadores pelo correio; as doações nos albergues.
É impossível portar soluções para todas as questões. Carregamos o essencial e lidamos com as situações à medida que vão se apresentando. "Menos é mais" tornou-se o jargão das conversas que, junto com as bolhas nos pés, alimentava muitos dos assuntos emergentes. No mais, era preciso aprender a secar as bolhas, aplicar iodo dentro delas, vestir duas meias para evitar a fricção com a umidade e parar, por quinze minutos, a cada duas horas, para secar pés e meias.

Ser documentarista despertava a curiosidade de muitos. De onde eu era? O que eu faria com as imagens?
Logo percebi que a abertura das pessoas às minhas lentes exigia de mim uma permuta.
Na maioria das vezes, nos hospedávamos em pequenos hotéis, pois o toque de recolher dos albergues impunha um sério obstáculo às tarefas no fim do dia.
Quando possível, o pernoite era feito em pequenas vilas em detrimento das cidades. Afinal, na rota destes dois metropolitanos, a preferencial era sempre das áreas menos habitadas.
Outra escolha que fiz foi pedalar por trilhas ao invés do asfalto. Diferentemente das longas distâncias percorridas pela maioria dos ciclistas, meu deslocamento era curto e exploratório.
A paz de espírito proporcionada pelas trilhas vinha acompanhada do desafio do peso das bagagens confrontando terreno, altimetria e velocidade.
Com a percepção plena ativada, buscava reduzir riscos de acidentes. As duas mãos sempre no guidão até Santiago me intuíam: "confie em Deus, mas amarre seu camelo".
Substituí óculos escuros pela aba do boné, fundamental para manter o foco e proteger contra o excesso de luz. Uma semi *dark room* em meio a tanto estímulo visual, através da qual eu filtrava o mundo acelerado.
Misticamente, depois que pendurei a Concha de Saint-Jacques, um dos símbolos do Caminho, no selim da bicicleta em Ponferrada, me senti mais alinhado e no fluxo da peregrinação. Possivelmente, renovei a tradição espontânea de muitos que seguiram estes rumos antes de mim ao longo dos últimos séculos.
E aqui viria à tona mais um ajuste de foco: a percepção da energia de proteção deixada por aqueles que por ali peregrinaram anteriormente.
Creio que por meio dessa energia surgem os Anjos do Caminho, que sincronicamente aparecem, ajudam e seguem. Chegam, partem.
Desde Portomarín, observei um aumento significativo no fluxo de pessoas. Os chamados "turisgrinos" juntavam-se a nós para percorrer os últimos cem quilômetros, impulsionados pela Compostela, o certificado oferecido na conclusão do Caminho.
O frescor dessa turma do trecho final contrastava com o semblante e a atitude de quem já vinha caminhando por centenas de quilômetros. Distinguiam-se as bagagens materiais e imateriais dos itinerantes que, finalmente, estavam chegando a Santiago.
Alcançamos nosso objetivo num domingo e presenciei um choque escancarado de realidades: peregrinos e turistas

misturados na Plaza do Obradoiro, felizes por terem chegado ao seu destino, independentemente dos meios utilizados. O que era essencial para um parecia ser sem razão para o outro.
Peregrinos se reencontrando, relembrando histórias e situações compartilhadas, agradecendo por terem chegado até ali.
Momento aguardado. Promessa realizada.
Alguns reviam família e amigos depois de caminhar por meses. Gente ajoelhada, chorando, rindo, tirando fotos, documentando sua conquista.
Gente contemplativa, absorta em outras dimensões.
E agora?

EL BICIGRINO Y EL PEREGRINO (2015)

El entrenador físico Aulus Sellmer me invitó a documentar su peregrinación por el Camino de Santiago en 2015. El viaje era parte del proyecto Desafíos por el Mundo, en el que enviaba boletines diarios a las emisoras de radio Eldorado y Estadão (São Paulo, Brasil) relatando sus experiencias durante el recorrido.
Por cuestiones de logística, ya que tenía que llevar diferentes equipos, elegí ir en bicicleta. Él fue a pie.
Y así acabamos formando una pareja poco común – él, peregrino, y yo, bicigrino.
Él había salido de Saint-Jean-Pied-de-Port, comienzo del Camino Francés. Nos encontramos a 300 km de allí, en Burgos, desde donde seguimos juntos hasta Santiago de Compostela, 500 km más adelante que recorrimos en 21 días.
En cuanto nos encontramos, Aulus me puso al corriente de la cultura del Camino que había ido acumulando.
La principal recomendación era librarse de cualquier peso superfluo, así que, desde el principio, hubo una constante reorganización de equipos, accesorios y objetos personales y los consiguientes envíos liberadores por correo, sin contar lo que iba dejando en los albergues.
No es posible cargar con soluciones para todos los imprevistos, llevamos lo esencial y manejamos las situaciones a medida que van surgiendo. "Menos es más" era un lema típico en las conversaciones que, así como las ampollas en los pies, estaba siempre presente.
Por lo demás, había que aprender a secar las ampollas aplicando yodo sobre ellas, poniéndose dos calcetines para evitar la fricción con la humedad y parar quince minutos cada dos horas para secarse tanto los pies como los calcetines.
Ver a un documentalista despertaba la curiosidad de mucha gente. ¿De dónde era? ¿Qué haría con las imágenes? Inmediatamente me di cuenta de que si quería que las personas se relajasen ante mi objetivo tendría que darles algo a cambio.
La mayoría de las veces nos hospedábamos en pequeños hostales, ya que en los albergues existe un horario de cierre y eso era un grave obstáculo para cumplir nuestras tareas al final del día. Siempre que era posible, pernoctábamos en pueblos en lugar de hacerlo en ciudades, pues, al fin y al cabo, en el camino de estos dos metropolitanos la preferencia la tienen zonas menos pobladas.
Otra decisión que se tomó fue la de pedalear por senderos en lugar de hacerlo por el asfalto. A diferencia de la mayoría de los ciclistas, que recorrían largas distancias, mis desplazamientos eran cortos y exploratorios. La paz de espíritu que los caminos proporcionaban venía acompañada del reto de superar el conflicto entre el peso del equipaje, el terreno, la altitud y la velocidad.
Era necesario estar atento a todo para reducir el riesgo de accidentes. Las dos manos siempre en el manillar hasta Santiago me hacían intuir: "confía en Dios, pero haz tu parte". Sustituí las gafas de sol por la visera de mi gorra, fundamental para mantener el enfoque y protegerme del exceso de luz. Una especie de cámara semioscura en medio de tanto estímulo visual y a través de la cual filtraba el mundo acelerado.
Místicamente, después de que colgué la *Coquille de Saint-Jacques* en el sillín de la bicicleta en Ponferrada, me sentí más estructurado y formando parte del flujo del Camino. Posiblemente, renové la espontánea tradición de muchos que anduvieron por aquí antes de mí a lo largo de los últimos siglos. Y aquí surgió un nuevo ajuste de enfoque: el de notar la energía protectora que dejaron aquellos que peregrinaron antes que nosotros.
Creo que de esta energía provienen los Ángeles del Camino que, sincrónicamente, aparecen, nos ayudan y siguen. Llegan y se van.
Desde Portomarín observé un aumento significativo en el flujo de personas. Eran los llamados *turisgrinos* que se nos unían para recorrer los últimos cien kilómetros impulsados por conseguir la Compostela, certificado que reconoce que se ha completado el Camino. El aspecto fresco del grupo del tramo de llegada contrastaba con el semblante y la actitud de aquellos que habían estado caminando cientos de kilómetros. Se distingue perfectamente el equipaje material e inmaterial de los diferentes caminantes que finalmente están llegando a Santiago.
Alcanzamos nuestro objetivo un domingo en el que fui testigo de un choque indiscutible de realidades. Peregrinos y turistas mezclados en la Plaza del Obradoiro, contentos

de haber llegado a su destino, independientemente del medio utilizado. Lo que para unos era esencial, para otros parecía no tener sentido.
Peregrinos volviéndose a encontrar, recordando historias y situaciones compartidas, agradecidos por haber llegado allí. Momento esperado. Promesa realizada.
Algunos se reunían con su familia y amigos después de caminar durante meses. Gente arrodillada, llorando, riendo, sacando fotos, registrando su logro. Gente contemplativa, absorta en otras dimensiones.
¿Y ahora qué?

THE BIKEGRIM AND THE PILGRIM (2015)

I was invited by Aulus Sellmer – accredited physical trainer and one of the creators of the project "Desafios pelo Mundo" – to document his pilgrimage through El Camino de Santiago, in 2015.
During the journey, he sent daily stories to Eldorado and Estadão radio stations, in São Paulo, recounting his experiences along the Camino.
For practical reasons, due to the equipment I needed to carry, I decided to ride a bike. He made the journey on foot. Thus, we became an unusual duo: myself, a "bikegrim"; and he, a pilgrim.
He departed from Saint-Jean-Pied-de-Port and I only joined him 300 km further on, in Burgos, from where we continued together to Santiago, traveling 500 km in 21 days.
As soon as we met, Aulus filled me in on the *Camino* culture he had gleaned, – stories, symbols and everything else learned from walking.
Getting rid of superfluous weight was the main recommendation. So, from the beginning, there was a constant reorganization of equipment, accessories and personal belongings, sending things back to Santiago de Compostela by mail, and donating items to hostels.
It's impossible to have a solution for every situation; we carried the essentials and handled problems as they emerged. "Less is more" became a typical topic of conversations, as blisters. Furthermore, the pilgrims had to learn how to dry out the blisters, applying iodine, wearing two pairs of socks to avoid friction with moisture, and stopping for fifteen minutes every two hours to dry both feet and socks.
Being a documentary filmmaker aroused the curiosity of many. Where did I come from? What was I going to do with the images? I soon realized that in order to get people to open up to my lens, I would have to barter.
Most of the time, we stayed in small hotels, as the curfew imposed by the hostels was a serious obstacle to our work at the end of the day. Whenever possible, we spent the night in villages rather than towns, as we preferred less populated areas.
I also decided to ride on pathways instead of asphalt. Unlike the long distances covered by most cyclists, my travels were short and exploratory. The peace of mind the trails provided came, however, with the challenge of overcoming the conflict between the weight of the luggage, the terrain, altitude and speed.
Fully aware of these facts, I tried to reduce the risk of accidents. Both hands always on the handlebars all the way to Santiago proved it: "Trust in God, but do your part." I replaced my sunglasses with a visor cap to help maintain focus and protect against excess light, which acted like a semi-dark room in the midst of many visual stimuli, through which I filtered the fast-paced world.
Quite mystically, after having attached the Santiago pilgrim shell to the saddle of my bike in Ponferrada, I felt more aligned and in flow with the *Camino*. It seemed to me that I had renewed the spontaneous tradition of those who had walked these trails before me for centuries past. This came with another adjustment of my focus: becoming aware of the protective energy left by those who pilgrimaged before us.
I believe that from this energy come the Angels of the *Camino*, who coincidently appear, help us, and leave.
They come and then depart.
After Portomarín, I noticed a significant increase in the flow of people. They were the so-called tourist pilgrims who joined us to walk the last one hundred kilometers, motivated by the Compostela, the certificate that recognizes that the *Camino* has been completed. The fresh look of the group on the final stretch was in stark contrast with the countenance and attitude of those who had been walking hundreds of kilometers.
The material and immaterial baggage of the different wanderers who finally arrive in Santiago were perfectly distinguishable.
We reached our goal on a Sunday, and I witnessed a blatant clash of realities. Pilgrims and tourists mingled in the Plaza do Obradoiro, both happy with their achievement or presence, regardless of the means they had used. What was essential for one seemed unreasonable for the other.
Pilgrims seeing each other again, remembering stories and experiences shared, grateful for having come so far.
A long-awaited moment. A promise made good.
Some reunited with relatives and friends after walking for months. People kneeling, crying, laughing, taking pictures, documenting their accomplishment.
People contemplating, absorbed in other dimensions.
And now what?

1- Spanish expression for Saint James Way

AULUS SELLMER

"Vou andar esses 780 km do Caminho de Santiago e, quem sabe, ficar mais perto de Deus" Em menos de um mês, o projeto dessa longa jornada estava pronto e eu a iniciava desde Saint-Jean-Pied-de-Port, na França, até Santiago de Compostela, na Espanha.
Com alguns dias do início da caminhada, minha percepção começou a mudar e passei a viver a peregrinação com outro olhar.
A mente foi compreendendo, passo a passo, que a fé move montanhas. Que a fé não se explica, transforma. Há diversas montanhas dentro de nós que precisam ser transpostas. Isso me levou a olhar para dentro e a aprender, ao observar meus próprios pensamentos, que era possível conversar com a alma. E, posso afirmar, isso é profundamente transformador.
É como manter consigo um diálogo íntimo e constante para poder prosseguir, independentemente do que vier pela frente.
No Caminho, não faltaram razões para desistir. Bolhas nos pés, o calor insuportável do verão espanhol, o peso da mochila nas costas, as longas distâncias entre um albergue e outro, noites maldormidas e cansaço extremo parecem obstáculos corriqueiros numa trajetória como essa, mas, quando se apresentam pela primeira vez, podem nos fazer desmoronar numa onda de pessimismo, estagnação e até de desistência.
Ao longo do percurso, ouvindo os peregrinos, minhas maneiras de pensar e agir foram se transformando. Relatos de superação, de entrega e de cooperação mútua me levaram a refletir de verdade.
Eu me conscientizei, por exemplo, de que viver não requer a posse de muitos bens materiais e pode ser muito mais rico quando acompanhado de desapego.
Por mais óbvia que essa constatação pareça, a imersão nas ocupações cotidianas faz esse tipo de percepção escapar. A agilidade conveniente do automatismo nos afasta do discernimento.
Compreendi também que as dificuldades não surgem por acaso.
Elas se revelam por algum motivo, como o de não desistir dos propósitos da vida.
Quem, hoje, em meio ao movimento constante, consegue dedicar 26 dias à reflexão?
Quando muito, reservamos algumas poucas horas, ou parcos minutos, dentro da rotina.
Reavaliei muitas coisas, ponderando sobre o que de fato realizei.
Entendi, aos 56 anos, que os valores podem mudar, que nunca é tarde para tomar decisões importantes e escolher novos caminhos.
Aprendi a ser menos apegado, a deixar de ser ranzinza e a não desistir diante da primeira dificuldade.
Nunca esqueço que, quando cheguei à Catedral de Santiago de Compostela, após percorrer 780 km em 26 dias, meu primeiro pensamento foi o de voltar, mesmo tendo acabado de concluir a peregrinação.
E foi o que fiz, dois anos depois.

Buen Camino.

"Voy a recorrer esos 780 km del Camino de Santiago y quién sabe si acercarme un poco más a Dios". En menos de un mes, el proyecto estaba listo y yo emprendía la jornada de Saint-Jean-Pied-de-Port, en Francia, a Santiago de Compostela, en España.
Después de algunos días caminando, mi primera idea fue cambiando y empecé a ver la peregrinación de otra forma. Mi mente fue comprendiendo que la fe mueve montañas.
Cada uno tiene varias montañas dentro de sí que hay que conquistar. Eso me condujo a hacer un trabajo de introspección y a aprender con los pensamientos que podía conversar con el alma. Lo que puedo asegurar es que es algo transformador.
Es como mantener una conversación en profundidad con uno mismo para continuar sin importar lo que venga por delante.
A lo largo del Camino no faltaron razones para desistir. Las ampollas en los pies, el calor insoportable del verano español, el peso de la mochila en la espalda,

las largas distancias entre los albergues, noches mal dormidas y cansancio extremo parecen problemas habituales de un itinerario como este, pero, cuando surgen, muchas veces lo que hacemos al primer revés es caer en el pesimismo y quedarnos estáticos.
Incluso llegamos a desistir.
Durante el recorrido, mi forma de pensar y de actuar fue cambiando al escuchar a los peregrinos. Relatos de superación, entrega y cooperación mutua me hicieron reflexionar. Una de las cosas de las que me hice consciente, por ejemplo, es que no se necesitan muchos bienes materiales para vivir, y que la vida puede aprovecharse mucho mejor cuando somos desprendidos.
Puede parecer obvio, pero cuando estamos inmersos en nuestras ocupaciones cotidianas esto es algo que no notamos, se nos escapa. La agilidad conveniente del automatismo nos aleja del discernimiento.
También comprendí que las dificultades no ocurren porque sí, sino que tienen una razón de ser, como la de no desistir de los propósitos de la vida.
¿Quién dispone hoy de 26 días para pensar y estar en movimiento? Como mucho, reservamos algunas horas de nuestra rutina diaria. Esto me hizo replantearme muchas cosas y reflexionar sobre lo que había realizado.
A los 56 años entendí que los valores pueden cambiar, que nunca es tarde para tomar decisiones importantes y para elegir nuevos caminos. Aprendí que se puede ser más desprendido, dejar de ser gruñón y no desistir ante la primera dificultad.
Nunca me olvido de que cuando llegué a la Catedral de Santiago de Compostela, después de 780 km en 26 días, el primer pensamiento que me vino a la mente fue el de repetir, a pesar de haber acabado de terminar la peregrinación, algo que volví a hacer dos años después.

Buen Camino

"I'm going to walk those 780 km of *El Camino de Santiago* and maybe, who knows, get a little bit closer to God."
In less than a month, the project was setup, and I left from Saint-Jean-Pied-de-Port in France to Santiago de Compostela in Spain.
After a few days of walking, my perception slowly began to change and I started to experience the pilgrimage in a different light. My mind began to understand that faith does move mountains.
There are many mountains within us that we need to be conquered. This made me look inside and realize that through my thoughts I could converse with my soul, and that is for sure very transformative.
It's like having a deep conversation with oneself in order to keep going, no matter what may lie ahead.
Along the *Camino* there were many reasons to give up. Blisters on the feet, the unbearable heat of the Spanish summer, the weight of the backpack, long distances between hostels, bad sleeping, and extreme fatigue seem like common problems to this type of hiking. However, when they do arise, they often sweep us away in a wave of despair and pessimism, even to the point of giving up.
Yet, listening to other pilgrims changed my way of thinking and acting. Stories of overcoming obstacles, determination, and helping each other really made me think. I realized, for example, that life can be better enjoyed with fewer possessions and more dettachment.
Although this insight may seem cliché, when we are immersed in daily occupations this sort of perception escapes us. Convenient automatism takes away discernment.
I also realized that difficulties do not come up by chance. They may cross our path to make us not give up, for example.
Being constantly busy, who can devote 26 days to reflection? At best, we reserve a few hours in our daily routine for it. This made me think over on what I had accomplished.
At 56, I finally understood that values can change; that is never too late to make important decisions and choose new paths. I learned to be less attached, to stop being grumpy, and not to give up at the first setback.
I shall never forget that, when I arrived at the Cathedral of Santiago de Compostela, after walking 780 km in 26 days, my first thought was to do it again, even though I had just finished the pilgrimage – and I did it, two years later.

Buen Camino

A EXPERIÊNCIA COM CLAUDIA (2017)

Decidi voltar ao Caminho com um novo propósito: transformar em livro as imagens feitas durante a peregrinação ciclística com Aulus Sellmer, em 2015. Para isso, era preciso complementar os registros.
Parte do meu treinamento pré-viagem consistiu em fazer longas caminhadas por São Paulo, carregando livros nas costas.
A necessidade de estar alerta numa cidade tensa como esta contribuiu para aprimorar a prática da meditação ativa. O instinto de autoproteção ativou um estado de prontidão muito semelhante ao que permearia a jornada que estava por vir.
Claudia Oliva participou da preparação, afinal estávamos prestes a realizar a caminhada juntos.
Saímos de Saint-Jean-Pied-de-Port e fomos até Castrojeriz em 2017. Fizemos 300 km em 19 dias.
Com o Aulus, de bicicleta, conheci "o fim"; agora, com a Claudia, faria "o começo" do Caminho Francês a pé. Uma inversão natural.
Caminhando, constatei que essa é a forma mais natural de peregrinar. Andar nos coloca em contato direto com a terra. Sem intermediários. Uma simples ação que refina as formas de agir e de pensar.
Existe uma relação clara e proporcional: quanto maior a quantidade de passos, maior a proximidade com os instintos.
A intensa experiência multissensorial promovida pela travessia dos Pirineus marca o início do Caminho. O frescor do Antigo Mundo se acentua nas narinas e na impressão dos olhos sobre a natureza deslumbrante. As formas espiraladas, moldadas pelas intempéries ao longo dos séculos, se refletem nos pelos dos animais, nas plantas e nos contornos das montanhas — uma dança silenciosa entre o que é mínimo e o que é imenso, em perfeita sintonia com o bioma que os abriga.
Vidas elementais se mostram sempre muito presentes.
Ali conhecemos o amigo-peregrino Brahma.
O contato com a energia ancestral das cores chancelava na memória laranjas, vermelhos, marrons e verdes em abundantes e inéditas combinações de formas e matizes.
O clima era seco. Não havia desperdício.
Resiliência.
Era o Caminho se apresentando.
Esse foi o cenário do primeiro jantar comunitário no Refúgio Orisson e da primeira missa dos peregrinos na Catedral de Roncesvalles.
Navarra e La Rioja mesclam as línguas espanhola e basca com as culturas do azeite, do vinho e do pimentão.
Uvas e olivas vicejam geometricamente sobre os morros.
Nas reuniões de familiares e amigos à beira da estrada, os diálogos animados se entrelaçam aos pimentões, como ingredientes numa receita afetuosa. No calor da chama e da conversa, tornam-se iguarias — da alma e da mesa — moldadas pelas mãos que, com delicadeza, retiram a pele e as sementes do fruto.
Uma profusão de culturas locais se oferece àqueles que atravessam a região e entram nos vilarejos de onde os jovens partiram e onde, agora, os idosos adicionam às bagagens dos peregrinos infindáveis conversas.
Esses encontros com os mais velhos aconteciam nos passeios matinais, antes que os ares amenos dessem lugar ao calor intenso.
Nesses dias, em diversos sentidos, íamos trocando de camadas e, no literal, nos despindo das vestimentas, no decorrer das horas e do movimento. A combinação de cores, formatos e tecidos inventava a improvável Moda do Caminho.
Em muitos dias, o calor tinha o poder de fazer o cenário latejar.
Achar uma fonte d'água caía tão bem como a ideia de uma chuva.
O deslocamento em certos horários e temperaturas era determinante para encontrar tudo vazio e cruzar as vilas fantasmas impossibilitava a reposição do farnel.
É notória a diferença entre sede e fome. A fome se posterga, a sede desnorteia.
A sede permeia o corpo. Um desconforto que mexe com o jeito de se sentir o mundo.
Ao atravessar áreas descampadas, em preparo para o plantio, passamos longas horas sem água e na companhia de um grupo de irlandeses esfuziantes,

justamente no dia em que passamos pela Vinícola de Irache e seu manancial de vinho.
A redenção veio com um dos peregrinos mais avançados do grupo, que alcançou o vilarejo de Los Arcos e regressou trazendo-nos uma garrafa d´água gelada. Gesto memorável!
É gratificante participar da interdependência gerada pela vulnerabilidade compartilhada.
Expostos e reunidos.
Mais adiante, a Oração de São Francisco voltou a fazer sentido na minha vida. Num encontro com alguns poucos peregrinos, o padre Manuel Garcia, da Igreja de Belorado, pediu a mim e à Claudia para que a lêssemos em português.
No Caminho, o sentido de congregar cumpre uma rota que independe de conotação religiosa.

LA EXPERIENCIA CON CLAUDIA (2017)

Decidí volver al Camino movido por el deseo de hacer este libro a partir de las fotografías de la peregrinación que realicé en bicicleta con Aulus Sellmer, en 2015,
y porque necesitaba completar las imágenes captadas.
Parte de mi entrenamiento consistía en dar largos paseos por São Paulo cargando libros a la espalda.
La necesidad de estar alerta en una ciudad tensa como São Paulo me ayudó a perfeccionar la práctica de la meditación activa. El instinto de autoprotección activó un estado de prontitud muy parecido al del viaje que iba a realizar.
Claudia Oliva también participó en esta preparación, ya que estábamos a punto de recorrer este Camino juntos.
Salimos de Saint-Jean-Pied-de-Port rumbo a Castrojeriz en 2017. Recorrimos 300 km en 19 días.
Con Aulus conocí "el fin" en bicicleta y, ahora, con Claudia, iba a hacer "el comienzo" del Camino Francés a pie. Una inversión normal.
Al caminar me di cuenta de que esta es la forma más natural de peregrinar. El andar nos pone en contacto directo con la tierra. Sin intermediarios. Una sencilla acción que refina las formas de actuar y pensar. En una relación clara y proporcional, cuantos más pasos se den, más se acerca uno a sus instintos.
La intensa experiencia multisensorial proporcionada por la travesía de los Pirineos señala el principio del Camino. El frescor del Antiguo Mundo se acentúa en el olfato y la mirada se ilumina ante una naturaleza deslumbrante.
La intemperie entalla el mundo animal, mineral y vegetal ofreciendo formas retorcidas consistentemente proyectadas por el tiempo y orquestadas por la íntima asociación entre los pelos de los animales y las montañas.
Vidas elementales siempre muy presentes.
Allí conocimos a Brahma, un amigo peregrino.
El contacto con la energía ancestral de los colores grababa en la memoria naranjas, rojos, marrones y verdes mezclados en profusión e inéditas combinaciones de formas y matices.
El clima era seco.
No había desperdicio.
Resiliencia.
Era el Camino que ya estaba presentándose.
En este escenario se desarrolló la primera cena comunitaria en Refugio Orisson y la primera misa de los peregrinos en la Catedral de Roncesvalles.
Navarra y La Rioja mezclan el castellano y el euskera con la cultura del aceite, el vino y el pimiento.
Uvas y olivas brillan geométricamente en las faldas de las montañas.
En las reuniones de parientes y amigos al borde de la carretera, interacciones y pimientos van transformándose en manjares en el alma y en el fuego, después de quitar pieles y semillas.
Una avalancha de culturas locales se pone a disposición de quienes cruzan la región y entran en los pueblos de los que salieron los jóvenes y donde abundan personas de avanzada edad que suman al equipaje de los peregrinos interminables conversaciones e imágenes.
Estos encuentros con los más mayores ocurrían durante su paseo por la mañana, antes de que subiera la temperatura y apretara el calor.
Durante esos días, en varios sentidos, íbamos quitándonos capas y desnudándonos, literalmente, con el paso de las horas y el movimiento. La combinación de colores, formas y tejidos inventaba la improbable Moda del Camino.
Muchos días, el calor hacía que el escenario ondulase.
Encontrar una fuente era tan bueno como imaginarse una lluvia.
Trasladarse a ciertas horas, o dependiendo de la temperatura, significaba encontrar todo vacío. Cruzar los pueblos fantasmas impedía reponer las provisiones.
Hay una marcada diferencia entre sed y hambre. El hambre se posterga, la sed desorienta. La sed atraviesa el cuerpo. Un malestar que afecta a la manera como uno siente el mundo.
Cruzando descampados que estaban siendo preparados

para el plantío, nos quedamos la mitad de un día sin agua junto a un grupo de irlandeses saltarines, justo el día que pasamos por la Vinícola de Irache y su fuente de vino.
La redención vino cuando uno de los peregrinos más avanzados del grupo llegó al pueblo de Los Arcos y regresó para traernos una botella de agua fría.
Un gesto memorable.
Es muy gratificante vivir esa interdependencia que se genera como fruto de la vulnerabilidad de todos.
Expuestos y reunidos.
Un poco más adelante, la Oración de San Francisco una vez más apareció en mi vida teniendo sentido. Durante un encuentro con pocos peregrinos, el padre Manuel García, de la Iglesia de Belorado, nos pidió a Claudia y a mí que la leyéramos en portugués.
En el Camino, el hecho de congregarse cumple una función independiente de cualquier connotación religiosa.

THE EXPERIENCE WITH CLAUDIA (2017)

I decided to go back to the Camino with a new purpose: to produce a book with pictures I shoot during the pilgrimage with Aulus Selmer in 2015. In order to do it, I should complement my records.
As part of my preparation for the second trip, I took long walks in São Paulo, carrying books on my back.
The need to be alert in a busy city like this helped me perfect the practice of active meditation. The instinct of self-preservation triggered a state of readiness very similar to what I would experience in the journey I was about to take.
Claudia Oliva joined in the preparations as we were going to walk the *Camino* together.
We left Saint-Jean-Pied-de-Port and towards Castrojeriz, covering 300 km in 19 days.
Cycling with Aulus, I knew "the end" of the French Way. Now, on foot with Claudia, I would know "the beginning" – a natural inversion.
Walking made me realize that this is the most natural way to go on a pilgrimage. On foot we are directly in touch with earth. No intermediaries. A simple movement refining actions and thoughts, in a clear and proportional relationship. The more steps you take, the closer you get to your instincts.
The intense multisensory experience of crossing the Pyrenees highlights the start of the journey. The Old World freshness is uniquely felt in the nostrils and the eyes are dazzled by the splendor of nature.
Spiral forms shaped by the rigorous weather throughout centuries echo on plants texture, animal hair patterns, and mountains – a silent dance between minimum and immense, in perfect harmony with the environment that houses them.
Elemental beings show everywhere.
This is where we met our pilgrim friend Brahma.
Being in touch with the ancestral energy of colors engraved the memory with shades of orange, red, brown, and green in abundant and never seen combinations of shapes and hues.
Dry weather.
No waste.
Resilience.
The *Camino* was introducing itself.
This was the setting for the first communal dinner at the Orisson Refuge and the first pilgrim mass at the Roncesvalles Cathedral.
Navarra and La Rioja combine Spanish and Basque languages with the culture of olive oil, wine, and peppers.
Grapes and olives grow abundantly in geometric patterns on the slopes.
While families and friends gather along the road, conversations and peeled and seedless bell pepers on the fire turn into delicacies for body and soul.
A profusion of local cultures is offered to those crossing the region and coming to the villages left by the young, where the elders add endless conversations to the pilgrims' baggages.
These encounters with the elders happened usually during their morning walks, before the coolness gives way to heat.
In many ways, on those days we shed layers. In the most literal way though, layers of clothes were took off over the course of hours and movements.
This combination of colors, shapes, and fabrics was creating a so called *Camino* fashion.
On many days, the heat made the scenery throb. Discovering a fountain used to sound as wonderful as a rainfall.
Walking at certain hours and the heat meant finding every place deserted. Crossing ghost towns prevented replenishing supplies.
There is a marked difference between thirst and hunger. Hunger can be ignored, but thirst needs quenching. It takes hold of your body. The discomfort affects your perception of the world around you.
Crossing bare fields in preparation for planting, we spent long hours without water and accompanied by a lively

Irish group, precisely in the day we were approaching Irache's wine and its great fount of wine. Hours later, relief came thanks to one pilgrim of a more advanced group, who had reached the village of Los Arcos, and returned with a bottle of cold water.
What a memorable gesture!
It is very gratifying to experience that interdependence which results from everyone's vulnerability. All exposed and yet united.
A little later, the prayer of St. Francis once again gave meaning to my life. In a meeting with a few pilgrims, Father Manuel Garcia, from the church of Belorado, asked Claudia and myself to read the prayer in Portuguese.
On the *Camino*, the act of gathering plays a role that is independent of any religious connotation.

CLAUDIA OLIVA

Quando fui convidada para fazer o Caminho, não imaginava o que viria pela frente.
Nunca tive um chamado, como outros peregrinos que buscam uma resposta, um norte, uma vivência espiritual ou mesmo uma experiência esportiva.
Fui convidada pelo fotógrafo Eduardo Quintino, que já havia feito o Caminho de bike. Dessa vez, ele queria voltar e, assim, registrar novas imagens para publicar um livro com a sensível narrativa visual que documentara em parte do percurso.
A beleza de suas fotos e a ótima companhia do Eduardo me atraíram a aceitar o convite.
A ideia, além de acompanhá-lo, era fazer algumas pinturas para minha coleção de aquarelas de viagem.
Com o passar dos dias e a dinâmica das caminhadas, uma mágica foi acontecendo e transformando minha percepção do mundo e dos meus sentimentos.
Acordar antes do sol nascer e andar até ele se pôr, dia após dia, entre campos, florestas e plantações de oliveiras, uvas e girassóis, passou a me trazer paz e uma nova perspectiva do tempo.
Um tempo necessário para ver a escuridão da noite se tornar luz, para entregar o dia ao seu rumo.
O tempo dos ciclos da vida tecia sem pressa uma nova surpresa com a afluência de cores e tonalidades no céu. Na atmosfera do outono, embarcavam folhas alaranjadas e vermelhas, enquanto a terra aguardava uma nova germinação.
Tempo de espera, de refletir, andar, respirar. Tempo de renascer.
As manhãs começavam geladas, aqueciam com o passar das horas, até o corpo suar e se acostumar com a caminhada. No mesmo ritmo, como numa sinfonia, em que cada timbre tem sua estreia, pássaros, borboletas e outros bichinhos faziam suas entradas.
Os pensamentos, que no começo do Caminho eram tantos, ficavam para trás, cediam ao silêncio da contemplação do belo: a natureza com suas cores, seus cheiros, frescores e movimentos.
Percebíamos o corpo, as limitações, as conquistas.
Descobríamos que é ao presente que pertencemos.
Sem TV, política, trânsito, carro, à mercê do tempo que os pés podiam levar.
As pessoas que cruzávamos nos desejavam um "Buen Camino". Isso fazia toda a diferença, soava como uma bênção de peregrino para peregrino, de irmão para irmão. Uma irmandade em torno dos encontros, desencontros e, muitas vezes, reencontros consumados com grande alegria.
Não há como seguir adiante carregando tantas coisas na alma e no coração. Aos poucos, vamos largando as mochilas pesadas e (re)conhecendo a leveza.
Os peregrinos compartilham com prazer o pouco que carregam. Temos todos as mesmas necessidades, os mesmos pés machucados e corpos doloridos, a mesma sede – e a mesma paz – de quem está trilhando um caminho sem volta. O outro, seja quem for, é um conforto. É cúmplice.
Experimentamos, assim, a empatia.
Ninguém pergunta qual é a sua religião, qual carro você tem, em quem votou. Nada disso condiz com o Caminho. O sorriso vem fácil, a troca cultural engrandece e alimenta as vivências individuais e coletivas. As diferenças aproximam.

E, assim, experimentamos a simpatia.
Nos albergues, dormimos todos sob um mesmo teto, às vezes em mosteiros ou em antigas construções.
Nas ruínas de um templo sagrado, visitamos um dos albergues mais acolhedores e ali tivemos a honra de apreciar as estrelas entre as paredes desmoronadas.
Nesses lugares, com frequência a comida e o vinho são partilhados em meio a confraternizações com música, conversas profundas e momentos de cura para as dores do corpo e da alma.
Os vários idiomas vão se misturando na alquimia de uma linguagem acessível a todos, carinhosa e divertida.
Dessa forma se reproduz a "Santa Ceia".
Embora eu não seja uma pessoa religiosa, acredito que o pensamento Cristão compactue com a ideia de aceitarmos e acolhermos o outro como irmão.
De percebermos que, de fato, fluímos todos na mesma direção.
Na minha opinião, esse é o grande milagre do Caminho: ali vivemos o melhor do ser humano. As catedrais e antigos templos de oração e iniciação espalhados pelo percurso contribuem para essa reflexão.
A grandeza dos edifícios e a riqueza da simbologia mística de diferentes linhas de pensamento nos colocam em nosso pequeno lugar e seguimos com mais humildade.
Reconhecemos que nada sabemos.
O Caminho de Santiago, o Caminho das Estrelas, transformou minha vida trazendo de volta a fé na humanidade; eu a havia perdido.
Ao me fazer olhar para dentro, me apresentou um novo lado de fora.
Jamais esquecerei essa oportunidade de aproximação com a parcela divina que está em todos nós, no tempo e no espaço. No presente.
E por esse presente, Edu, te agradeço com todo o meu coração.
Que essa luz guie sempre o seu caminho.

Cuando recibí la invitación para hacer el Camino, no podía ni imaginar lo que me esperaba.
Nunca sentí un impulso como otros peregrinos que buscan una respuesta, un norte, una vivencia espiritual o incluso una experiencia deportiva.
Quien me invitó fue Eduardo Quintino, fotógrafo que ya había hecho el Camino en bicicleta y tenía el objetivo de volver y captar más imágenes para su proyecto de publicar un libro que registrase su mirada fascinante sobre el recorrido.
La belleza de sus fotos y la excelente compañía de Eduardo hicieron que aceptase la invitación.
Además de acompañarlo, la idea era hacer algunas pinturas para mi colección de acuarelas de viaje.
Con el transcurso de los días y la dinámica de las caminatas, mi percepción del mundo y de mis sentimientos fue cambiando como por arte de magia.
Despertar antes del amanecer y andar hasta la puesta del sol durante días y días por campos, bosques y tierras sembradas con olivos, vides y girasoles fue transmitiéndome una sensación de paz y una nueva percepción del tiempo. Un tiempo que es necesario para que la oscuridad de la noche se transforme en luz y haga que el día siga su rumbo.
El tiempo de los ciclos de la vida tejía sin prisa una nueva sorpresa con profusión de colores y tonalidades en el cielo. La atmósfera del otoño cargaba hojas anaranjadas y rojizas, mientras que la tierra esperaba una nueva germinación.
Tiempo de espera, de reflexión, de andar y respirar.
Tiempo de renacer.
Las mañanas comenzaban muy frías y la temperatura iba subiendo con las horas, el cuerpo comenzaba a sudar y a acostumbrarse al caminar. Al mismo ritmo, como en una sinfonía en la que cada timbre tiene su estreno, pájaros, mariposas y otros bichitos iban entrando. Si al principio del Camino había muchos pensamientos, fueron quedándose atrás, dando lugar a un silencio que invitaba a la contemplación de lo bello: la naturaleza con sus colores, sus aromas, sus movimientos y su frescor.
Percibíamos nuestro cuerpo, limitaciones y logros.
Descubrimos que pertenecemos al tiempo presente.
Sin televisión, política, tráfico, coche, a merced del ritmo que nuestros pies nos permitían.
Las personas con las que nos vamos cruzando nos desean un "Buen Camino". Eso ya de por sí marca una gran diferencia, suena como una bendición de peregrino a peregrino, de hermano a hermano. Se forma una hermandad alrededor de los encuentros, desencuentros y, muchas veces, reencuentros llenos de una gran alegría.
No se puede seguir adelante cargando tantas cosas en el alma y en el corazón. Poco a poco vamos deshaciéndonos de pesadas mochilas y (re)conociendo la levedad. Los peregrinos comparten con gusto lo poco que llevan consigo. Todos tenemos las mismas necesidades, los mismos pies maltrechos y cuerpos doloridos, la misma sed y paz de quien avanza por un

camino sin vuelta. El otro, sea quien sea, nos reconforta. Es un cómplice.
Y así vamos sintiendo la empatía.
Nadie te pregunta cuál es tu religión, qué coche tienes o en quién has votado. Eso no cabe en el Camino. La sonrisa surge con facilidad, el intercambio cultural engrandece y alimenta las experiencias individuales y colectivas. Las diferencias nos acercan.
Y así vamos sintiendo la simpatía.
En los albergues, todos dormimos bajo un mismo techo, a veces en monasterios o construcciones antiguas.
En las ruinas de un templo sagrado encontramos uno de los albergues más acogedores y fue allí donde tuvimos el privilegio de ver las estrellas por entre las paredes desmoronadas. En esos lugares es frecuente compartir la comida y el vino en medio de una gran confraternización con derecho a cura de dolores, música y conversaciones profundas. Los diferentes idiomas se van mezclando en la alquimia de un lenguaje accesible a todos, cariñoso y divertido. De esta forma se reproduce la "Santa Cena".
A pesar de no ser una persona religiosa, creo que el pensamiento cristiano va de eso, de aceptar y acoger al otro como hermano, de darse cuenta de que todos estamos en un mismo camino.
En mi opinión, ese es el gran milagro del Camino: en él vivimos lo mejor del ser humano. Las catedrales y los antiguos templos de oración e iniciación a lo largo del recorrido también nos conducen a esa reflexión. La grandeza de los edificios y la riqueza de la simbología mística de diferentes líneas de pensamiento nos ponen en nuestro pequeño lugar y así seguimos con más humildad. Sabemos que no sabemos nada.
El Camino de Santiago, el Camino de las Estrellas, transformó mi vida al devolverme la fe que había perdido en la humanidad. Al hacer que mirase hacia dentro, me presentó un nuevo lado de fuera.
Jamás olvidaré esa oportunidad de aproximación con la parte divina que está en todos nosotros, en el tiempo y en el espacio. En el presente.
Edu, te agradezco ese regalo con todo mi corazón.
Que esa luz guíe siempre tu camino.

When I was invited to walk the *Camino*, I had no clue of what would lay ahead.
I never had a calling, like other pilgrims looking for an answer, some guidance, a spiritual experience or even a sporting challenge.
The offer was made by Eduardo Quintino, a photographer who had already explored the *Camino* by bicycle and wanted to return and take more images for his project, in order to publish a book documenting his fascinating perspective of the route.
The beauty of his photos besides Eduardo being an excellent company made me accept the invitation.
In addition, I wanted to make some paintings for my collection of travel watercolors.
With the days passing by, the dynamics of the walk magically transformed my perception of the world and my feelings.
Waking up before sunrise and walking until sunset, day after day, across fields, forests, and plantations of olive trees, grapes and sunflowers made me feel in peace, in a new rythm. The time needed to watch the darkness of the night turning into the light of a new day on its own course. The time of the cycles of life was weaving with no rush surprising profusions of colors and shades in the sky. The autumn atmosphere was carrying orange and red leaves, while the soil was expecting new seedlings.
A time for waiting, meditating, walking and breathing.
A time for rebirthing.
Mornings were freezing and would warm up gradually, until the body sweated and got used to walking. In the same pace, like a symphony, tone by tone, birds, butterflies and other tiny animals were making their entrance. Thoughts, which there were so many at the beginning, were left behind, giving way to the silence that invites the contemplation of the beauty – nature and its colors, fragrances, movements and vitality.
We became aware of our body, our limits and achievements.
We realized that we belonged to the here and now.
No television, no politics, no traffic, no cars, at the mercy of our own steps.
People crossing our way wished us a *Buen Camino*. That makes a big difference. It sounds like a blessing from pilgrim to pilgrim, from brother to brother.
A brotherhood built around encounters, good-byes and frequent joyful reunions.
One cannot go forward carrying so many things in the heart and soul. Little by little, we were letting go heavy backpacks and (re)discovering lightness.
Pilgrims gladly share whatever they carry. We all have the same needs, the same battered feet and aching bodies, the same thirst and peace of those who walk a path with no return. The others, whoever they were, they comforted us. They were accomplices.

We could call it empathy.
No one asks what your religion is, what car you own or who you voted for. These things have no place on the *Camino*. Smiles come easily, and the cultural exchanges enhance and nourish individual and collective experiences. Differences bring people together.
We could call it sympathy.
We all slept under the same roof in the hostels and sometimes in monasteries and old buildings. In the ruins of a sacred temple, we found one of the most welcoming hostels; there we had the privilege of seeing the stars through the crumbling walls. In these places, food and wine are often shared while get-togethers, deep conversations and moments of physical and emotional healing are happening. Different idioms merge; a funny and lovely language accessible to everybody.
It feels like the "Lord's Supper".
Although I'm not a religious person, I do believe that Christian thinking is about accepting and welcoming others as brothers and sisters, realizing that we are all on the same path.
In my opinion, this is the great miracle of the *Camino* – to taste the best of humanity. All cathedrals and ancient temples of prayer and initiation along the route contribute to this reflection. The grandeur of the buildings and the richness of the mystical symbolism of different schools of thought bring us to our small place and then we can go on humbly. We realize that we know nothing.
The *Camino de Santiago*, the Path of the Stars, changed my life by restoring my faith in humanity, which I had lost. By making me look inward, it gave me a new outward perspective.
I shall never forget this opportunity to get closer to the divine part in all of us, in time and space.
In the present.
And for this gift, Edu, I thank you with all my heart.
May this light always guide your path.

Na página ao lado e nas seguintes, os encontros que marcaram a caminhada.

En la página contigua y en las siguientes, los encuentros que marcaron el camino.

On the next pages, the encounters that marked the journey.

Ireland

BERTRAND SAINT-MACARY

Meu envolvimento como médico no Caminho começou ao encontrar os peregrinos pela estrada no passado e hoje já faz trinta anos que coordeno a Associação de Peregrinos de Saint-Jean-Pied-de-Port.
Sempre andei muito por estas montanhas e conheço bem as repentinas mudanças climáticas da região. Por isso, assumi a missão de orientar sobre riscos, num território marcado por acidentes, desaparecimentos e mortes.
O peso excessivo das mochilas é outra preocupação recorrente. Procuro contribuir para que o pessoal reflita sobre a utilidade do que carrega, como um exercício constante de simplicidade e desapego.
Estas cadeias montanhosas guardam diversas memórias, entre elas a cópia do Códice Calistino, que fica em Saint Michel.
O manuscrito do século XII apresenta um detalhado guia de apoio ao peregrino, evidenciando que já coexistiam à época as intenções de penitência e do simples caminhar, assim como ocorre hoje, com a popularização da peregrinação.
Em 1975, contava-se menos de 10 peregrinos por ano na região. O fluxo só aumentou a partir de 1985, quando foram abertos albergues à base de doação. O Caminho, que antes interessava quase exclusivamente aos europeus, passou a atrair pessoas do mundo todo.

Mi colaboración como médico en el Camino comenzó hace tiempo, cuando empecé a encontrarme con peregrinos por la carretera, y ya llevo treinta años coordinando la Asociación de Peregrinos de Saint-Jean-Pied-de-Port.
Siempre he caminado mucho por estas montañas y conozco bien lo impredecible que puede ser el clima por aquí. Por eso decidí asumir la tarea de orientar sobre los riesgos que se corren en una zona donde, por desgracia, no han faltado accidentes, desapariciones y muertes.
El peso excesivo de las mochilas es otra de esas preocupaciones que se repiten. Intento ayudar a que la gente se plantee qué lleva consigo, como un ejercicio constante de sencillez y desapego.
Estas montañas guardan muchísimas historias. Una de ellas es la de la copia del Códice Calixtino que se conserva en Saint Michel.
Este manuscrito del siglo XII es una guía muy detallada para los peregrinos, en la que se pone en evidencia que ya en aquella época convivían las intenciones de hacer penitencia y el simple hecho de caminar, igual que ocurre hoy en día, ahora que la peregrinación se ha vuelto tan popular.
En 1975 únicamente pasaban por aquí diez peregrinos al año. El flujo se incrementó a partir de 1985, que es cuando se empezaron a abrir albergues gracias a las donaciones. El Camino, que antes prácticamente solo interesaba a los europeos, comenzó a atraer a personas de todas partes del mundo.

My role as a doctor on the Camino began when I interact with pilgrims on the roads in the past and now it has been 30 years since I've became head of the Saint-Jean-Pied-de-Port Pilgrims' Association.
I've been hiking on these mountains for a long time and I'm well aware of sudden climate changes in the region. Therefore, I took on the mission of warning the pilgrims about the risks in a territory known due to accidents, disappearances and deaths.
Overweight backpacks are another recurring concern. I try to help people think over the usefulness of what they are carrying as a constant exercise of simplicity and detachment.
These mountains hold many memories, including a copy of the Codex Calixtinus, which is kept in Saint Michel.
The 12th century manuscript presents a detailed guide to support pilgrims, showing that the intentions of penance and simple hiking already coexisted at the time, just as it occurs nowadays, with the popularization of pilgrimage.
In 1975, there was less than 10 pilgrims per year in the region. The flow only increased after 1985, when hostels were opened on a donation basis. The Camino, which initially had interested Europeans only, began to draw in people from all over the world.

BRAHMA

Vim ao Caminho porque precisava dar um tempo da vida.
Não sou um caminhante contumaz, mas me senti fascinado pela potencial conexão entre as pessoas quando seus corpos se movem lado a lado.
Costumo me deslocar bastante pela Europa e, no ano passado, quando visitei de carro Santiago de Compostela, fiquei magnetizado pelas pessoas e pela energia do Santo.
Ao entrar na Catedral, fui profundamente impactado pela vibração do lugar, e então catapultado às memórias dos templos hindus e suas construções grandiosas.
Há alguns meses, estive na Índia e compartilhei minhas inquietudes com uma amiga que me incentivou a fazer este Caminho.
Nesse país do sudeste asiático, encontrei almas sábias que me modificaram completamente, pessoas às quais me juntei e com quem vivi um processo de verdadeira mudança.
Elas me apresentaram Ramana Maharshi, ser iluminado cuja consciência despertou na montanha de Arunachala, na cidade de Tiruvannamalai, para onde muitas pessoas são atraídas, inclusive eu, que já estive lá 14 vezes.
Absorvidos por esse local sagrado, cada um se pergunta: quem sou eu?
Essa indagação estimula, e muito, minha escuta interna, despertando a noção de complementariedade entre o vazio e o amor que habitam cada indivíduo.

Vine al Camino porque necesitaba tomarme un respiro.
No soy un caminante contumaz, pero la potencial conexión entre personas que se mueven juntas fue algo que me atrapó.
Viajo bastante por Europa y, el año pasado, cuando fui a Santiago de Compostela me sentí atraído como por un imán por las personas y la energía del Santo.
Al entrar en la catedral, la vibración de aquel lugar me impactó de tal modo que me catapultó a los recuerdos de los templos hindúes y su grandiosidad.
Hace algunos meses estuve en India y, al compartir mis inquietudes con una amiga, ella me incentivó a recorrer el Camino.
En ese país del sudeste asiático encontré almas sabias que me cambiaron por completo, personas a las que me uní y acabaron transformándome.
Ellas me presentaron a Ramana Maharshi, ser iluminado cuya consciencia despertó en la montaña de Arunachala, en Tiruvannamalai, lugar que atrae a un gran número de personas, incluido yo, que ya fui catorce veces.
Cautivados por este lugar sagrado, cada uno se pregunta: ¿quién soy yo?
Esta indagación estimula mi escucha interior, despertando la noción de complementariedad entre el vacío y el amor intrínsecos a cada individuo.

I chose the *Camino* because I needed a break from life.
I'm not an eager walker, but I was fascinated by the potential community between people as their bodies move side by side.
I travel a lot around Europe and last year, when I visited Santiago de Compostela by car, I was mesmerized by the people and by the energy of the Saint. When I entered the Cathedral, I was struck by its vibrant energy, which took me back to my memories of Hindu temples and their grandiosity.
A few months ago, I had been to India and shared my restlessness with a friend who encouraged me to walk the *Camino*.
In this Southeast Asian country, I met wise souls who changed me completely; people I joined and together with whom I was transformed. They introduced me to Ramana Maharshi, an enlightened being whose consciousness awakened on the mountain of Arunachala in Tiruvannamalai, where many people are drawn to, including me. And I have gone there 14 times already.
When called to this sacred site, everyone asks oneself: Who am I?
This question stimulated my inner listening, awakening the notion of how emptiness and love, intrinsic to every individual, complement each other.

IVÁN ARCHIVOS

Meu nome é Iván Archivos, tenho 28 anos e já trabalhei como pintor, mecânico, motorista e, há três meses, decidi me dedicar a um empreendimento próprio.
Encontrei esta área próxima de Pamplona, pertencente a uma senhora de 70 anos, enquanto procurava um lugar para morar.
Entramos em um acordo e, em troca de uma modesta contribuição mensal, pude criar o *Olive Zen Garden*, esse espaço tranquilo de convivência entre oliveiras e área de descanso para acolher peregrinos.
Aqui ofereço tudo o que posso para acolher e dar conforto ao peregrino que passe e resolva parar.
Neste pedaço de terra, ainda sonho em plantar, criar animais e, quem sabe, viver aqui.
Também penso em ampliar o espaço e transformá-lo em uma hospedagem cultural, onde as pessoas possam descansar e se entreter com literatura.
Se essa ideia for boa também para as outras pessoas, então estou fazendo a coisa certa.

NOTA DO AUTOR: CONHECEMOS O *OLIVE ZEN GARDEN* E SEU ATENCIOSO IDEALIZADOR SOB A IMPRESSÃO DE QUE ESTÁVAMOS DIANTE DE UMA MIRAGEM – UM OÁSIS PARA CAMINHANTES ÁVIDOS POR UM "CAFUNÉ" GASTRONÔMICO LOGO CEDO, ENTRE OLIVEIRAS, FRUTAS FRESCAS, CASTANHAS, SUCO, BOLO E CAFÉ QUENTE ERAM GENEROSAMENTE OFERECIDOS EM TROCA DE DONATIVOS.

Me llamo Iván Archivos, tengo 28 años y he trabajado de pintor, mecánico y chófer, hasta que hace tres meses decidí dedicarme a algo mío.
Encontré este terreno cerca de Pamplona, que pertenece a una señora de 70 años, cuando estaba buscando un lugar para vivir.
Nos pusimos de acuerdo y, a cambio de una modesta contribución mensual, instalé el *Olive Zen Garden*.
Aquí ofrezco todo lo que puedo para acoger al peregrino que decida acercarse y hacer que se sienta cómodo.
También me gustaría plantar en este pedazo de tierra, criar animales y hasta llegar a vivir.
Pretendo ampliarlo y montar un parador cultural en el que las personas puedan descansar y entretenerse leyendo.
Y si esta idea es buena para otras personas, será que estoy haciendo lo correcto.

NOTA DEL AUTOR: CONOCIMOS EL *OLIVE ZEN GARDEN* Y A SU ATENTO CREADOR CUANDO NOS CRUZAMOS CON LO QUE PARECÍA SER UN ESPEJISMO PARA CAMINANTES ÁVIDOS DE UN MIMO GASTRONÓMICO. FRUTAS FRESCAS, CASTAÑAS, ZUMO, BIZCOCHO Y CAFÉ CALIENTE ERAN OFRECIDOS DE BUENA MAÑANA EN MEDIO DE LOS OLIVOS A CAMBIO DE LA VOLUNTAD.

My name is Iván Archivos, I'm 28 years old and I've worked as a painter, mechanic, driver, and, three months ago, I decided to start my own business.
I found this plot of land near Pamplona, while I was looking for a place to live. The owner is a 70-year-old lady. We came to an agreement and, in exchange for a modest monthly contribution, I was able to set up the *Olive Zen Garden*, where I offer everything I can to welcome and provide comfort to any pilgrim who passes by and decides to stop.
On this piece of land, I would still like to plant crops, raise animals, and possibly live.
I'm also thinking of expanding the space and turning it into a culture hostel, where people can rest and have access to a library.
If other people like this idea too, then I'm doing the right thing.

AUTHOR'S NOTE: WE VISITED THE OLIVE ZEN GARDEN AND ITS ENGAGED CREATOR AND WERE LEFT WITH THE IMPRESSION THAT IT WAS LIKE A MIRAGE FOR PILGRIMS EAGER FOR A GASTRONOMIC TREAT. EARLY IN THE MORNING, AMONG OLIVE TREES, FRESH FRUITS, CHESTNUTS, JUICES, CAKES, AND HOT COFFEE WERE OFFERED IN EXCHANGE FOR DONATIONS.

ÁUDIO DA CLAUDIA OLIVA FALANDO SOBRE IVÁN ARCHIVOS, APÓS NOSSO ENCONTRO COM ELE. (EM PORTUGUÊS COM LEGENDA EM PORTUGUÊS)

AUDIO DE CLAUDIA OLIVA HABLANDO SOBRE IVÁN ARCHIVOS DESPUÉS DEL ENCUENTRO CON ÉL. (EN PORTUGUÉS CON SUBTÍTULO EN ESPAÑOL)

LISTEN TO WHAT CLAUDIA OLIVA SAYS ABOUT IVÁN ARCHIVOS AFTER WE MET HIM. (IN PORTUGUESE WITH ENGLISH SUBTITLES)

NICOLÁS JIMÉNEZ AMADOR "CAMARÓN"

Sou Camarón, também me conhecem como o gari-cantor.
Trabalho pelas ruas de Estella, e enquanto varro, vou entoando canções ciganas que aprendi com minha família. E em qualquer trecho das vias que limpo faço dele um palco improvisado para a minha música.
Não conheço os autores de muitas das canções que me acompanham. Minha performance solitária e intensa lembra os Gipsy Kings, mas nasce da alma – só sei que as melodias, os cânticos, sempre estiveram comigo.
Em frente ao Albergue Municipal, converso com os peregrinos e às vezes busco na memória as manhãs da infância, quando minha irmã me acordava cantarolando.
De vez em quando, subo ao palco, este real, com meu irmão. Nós dois fazemos parte de um grupo musical da cidade.
Esse meu jeito diferente de trabalhar me rende, às vezes, um mosto — aquele sumo fresco da uva antes da fermentação — oferecido por algum morador generoso.
Nem a prefeitura nem meu chefe se incomodam com meu estilo de trabalhar. "Desde que esteja tudo limpo, está tudo certo", eles sempre me dizem.
Sigo assim, com voz, pá e vassoura, vivendo meu próprio ritual.

Soy Camarón, aunque también se me conoce como el barrendero cantante.
Trabajo en las calles de Estella y, mientras barro, voy entonando coplas que aprendí con mi familia, transformando cada trecho de aceras y calzadas que limpio en un escenario improvisado para presentar mis canciones.
No sé quiénes son los autores de muchas de las coplas que canto. Mi actuación solitaria e intensa recuerda a los Gipsy Kings, es algo que me sale de dentro –lo único que sé es que las melodías, las tonadas, siempre estuvieron conmigo.
Charlo con los peregrinos enfrente del albergue municipal y, a veces, busco entre mis recuerdos de pequeño las mañanas en que mi hermana me despertaba canturreando.
De vez en cuando, subo a un escenario de verdad con mi hermano. Formamos parte de un grupo de música local.
Esta manera diferente que tengo de trabajar hace que, esporádicamente, algún vecino generoso me ofrezca un mosto, ese zumo de uvas frescas extraído antes del proceso de fermentación.
Ni al ayuntamiento ni a mi jefe les molesta mi estilo de trabajar. "Mientras esté todo limpio, no hay de qué quejarse", dicen.
Y así voy marchando, a golpe de voz, recogedor y escobón, viviendo mi propio ritual.

I'm Camarón, also known as 'the singing street sweeper'.
I work on the streets of Estella, and while I sweep, I sing songs that I've learned from my family. I make up a stage for my music at any stretch of the roads I'm cleaning.
I don't know the authors of most of the songs I sing. My intense, solo performance is kind of reminiscent of Gipsy Kings, but it comes from the soul. I just know that the melodies and the lyrics have always been with me.
In front of the Municipal Hostel, chatting with the pilgrims, I sometimes recall some mornings in my childhood, when my sister used to wake me up humming.
Here and there I get on a stage – a real one – with my brother. We take part in a band in the city.
My peculiar way of working sometimes earns me a 'mosto' – that fresh grape juice extracted before fermentation – offered by a generous resident.
Neither the city hall or my boss are bothered by my work style, 'as long as everything is clean, it's all good' they say.
I keep going with my voice, a dustpan and a broom, carrying out my own ritual.

CONG YANG

Na Cruz de los Valientes, enquanto eu escrevia com calma no meu caderno, fui surpreendido por um fotógrafo. Ele se aproximou, curioso com a forma como eu registrava aquela experiência. Eu não imaginava que aquele momento renderia uma troca tão significativa.
Tenho visto muitas pessoas fazendo anotações ao longo do Caminho, mas o meu caderno era especial: um scrapbook que decidi preparar para uma amiga muito querida.
Havíamos combinado de fazer essa peregrinação juntos, mas, por conta de uma doença grave, ela não pôde vir.
Então, tenho vivenciado por ela a experiência que sonhamos juntos — e que agora registro, passo a passo, com imagens, palavras e também colagens.
Essa foto minha, com a mão na cruz, por alguma razão inspirou o fotógrafo, o Eduardo.
O curioso é que naquele dia voltamos a nos encontrar, sem combinarmos nada, quando eu estava ajudando na cozinha do albergue de Belorado.
Estou comemorando meus 30 anos andando sozinho — com preparo físico em dia, sem bolhas nos pés, e com o coração aberto para o que surgir. Gosto de admirar a paisagem e trocar histórias com os "Camino fellows".
Todos os dias, reservo cerca de uma hora e meia para compor, com dedicação, essa obra que, assim que estiver pronta, enviarei à minha amiga.

Estaba en la Cruz de los Valientes, escribiendo tranquilamente en mi cuaderno, cuando un fotógrafo me sorprendió. Él se acercó atraído por el modo en que estaba registrando esta experiencia.
En aquel momento, no me imaginaba lo que iba a suponer este intercambio.
Muchas personas hacen anotaciones a lo largo del Camino, pero mi cuaderno era especial: un álbum de recortes que decidí prepararle a una querida amiga.
Habíamos quedado en hacer la peregrinación juntos, pero ella no pudo venir por causa de una grave enfermedad.
Desde entonces, vivo por ella la experiencia que habíamos soñado hacer juntos —y que ahora registro, paso a paso, con imágenes, palabras y collage.
Esta foto en la que aparezco con la mano en la cruz, por alguna razón inspiro a Eduardo, el fotógrafo. Lo curioso es que aquel día volvimos a encontrarnos, de casualidad, cuando yo estaba ayudando en la cocina del albergue de Belorado.
Estoy celebrando mi trigésimo cumpleaños andando solo —en buena forma física, sin ampollas en los pies y con el corazón abierto a lo que surja. Me gusta contemplar el paisaje y compartir anécdotas con los compañeros del camino. Todos los días dedico cerca de una hora y media a componer de forma minuciosa esta obra y, una vez terminada, se la enviaré a mi amiga.

I was surprised by a photographer in Cruz de Los Valientes, while I was calmly writing in my notebook. He approached me interested about the way I was registering that experience. I would never have imagined that moment would result in such a remarkable exchange.
I've seen many people taking notes along The Camino, but my notebook was different – a scrapbook I was producing for a dear friend. We planned to make this trip together, but due to a serious illness, she was no longer able to come. So, I've been experiencing for her what we dreamed of together – I am reporting it step by step, with images, words and collages.
This photo of myself, with my hand on the cross, for some reason inspired the photographer, Eduardo. Curiously, we met again, without planning, when I was helping in the kitchen, at the hostel in Belorado.
I am celebrating my 30 th birthday by pilgriming alone – in good shape, no blisters on my feet, with my heart open to everything that crosses my path. I like to stare the landscape and exchange stories with the 'Camino fellows'. Every day, I dedicate about an hour and a half to carefully composing this work; as soon as I finish it, I will send it to my friend.

SANDRA TERRER

Fiz o Caminho no ano passado, começando sozinha a partir de Pamplona. Ao longo da peregrinação, conheci meu atual companheiro. Durante a jornada, nasceu em nós o desejo de servir os peregrinos, pois percebemos a oportunidade de um melhor atendimento. Voltamos à minha terra natal e logo regressamos ao Caminho, decididos a nos estabelecer por aqui.
Encontramos este paraíso chamado San Bol, onde atuo há cinco meses como hospitaleira, e com toda a dedicação que posso oferecer. Meu companheiro é cozinheiro em um albergue, na vizinha Hontanas del Camino. Aprendo muito com as pessoas que passam por aqui.
Para mim, alguém que deixa toda a comodidade para trás para carregar seus poucos pertences em mochilas durante semanas, já demonstra algo especial. Mesmo os que fazem o Caminho por etapas também revelam suas singularidades.
Muitos julgam os peregrinos como quem só está à procura de um turismo mais barato. Mas o peregrino é, na essência, um buscador, ainda que não saiba exatamente o que procura.
É alguém que não ignora suas inquietudes, mas as acolhe e caminha com elas.

NOTA DO AUTOR: CONHECI SANDRA DURANTE MINHA PRIMEIRA PEREGRINAÇÃO. QUANDO REGRESSEI AO CAMINHO DOIS ANOS MAIS TARDE, VOLTEI A PROCURÁ-LA, MAS ENCONTREI O ALBERGUE DE SAN BOL FECHADO.

Hice el Camino el año pasado. Salí sola de Pamplona y, durante la peregrinación, conocí a mi actual compañero.
A lo largo del recorrido fue surgiendo la idea de servir a los peregrinos porque veíamos que era posible mejorar la atención.
Volvimos a mi tierra natal y después regresamos al Camino para establecernos en él.
Encontramos este paraíso llamado San Bol y desde hace cinco meses trabajo lo mejor que puedo como hospitalera.
Mi compañero es cocinero en un albergue en la vecina Hontanas del Camino.
Aprendo mucho de las personas que pasan por aquí.
Para mí, una persona que deja su confort para atrás y va cargando sus pocas cosas en mochilas durante semanas, ya de por sí es alguien diferenciado. Incluso los que hacen el Camino por etapas son únicos.
Muchos ven a los peregrinos como personas que solo persiguen un turismo más barato. En realidad, el peregrino es un buscador, aunque no sepa lo que busca. Es alguien que en lugar de ignorar sus inquietudes las vive.

NOTA DEL AUTOR: CONOCÍ A SANDRA EN MI PRIMERA PEREGRINACIÓN. LA BUSQUÉ CUANDO REGRESÉ AL CAMINO, DOS AÑOS DESPUÉS, PERO ENCONTRÉ EL ALBERGUE DE SAN BOL CERRADO.

I walked the *Camino* last year, starting on my own from my hometown of Pamplona.
On the pilgrimage, I met my current partner.
During the journey, serving the pilgrims became a dream because we saw an opportunity to provide a better service.
We went back to Pamplona, but soon returned to the *Camino* to settle there. We found this paradise called San Bol, where I've been working as a hospitality worker for five months now. My partner is a cook in a hostel in nearby Hontanas del Camino.
I learn a lot from the people who pass through here.
For me, anyone who leaves all comforts behind to carry limited belongings in a backpack for weeks is special. Even those who walk the *Camino* in stages are unique.
Many people think of pilgrims as people who are just looking for cheap tourism. In reality, pilgrims are seekers, even if they don't know exactly what they're looking for. They don't ignore their worries, they choose to live them.

AUTHOR'S NOTE: I MET SANDRA ON MY FIRST PILGRIMAGE. I LOOKED FOR HER WHEN I RETURNED TO THE CAMINO TWO YEARS LATER, BUT THE SAN BOL HOSTEL WAS CLOSED.

VÍDEO DA SANDRA (FALADO EM ESPANHOL E LEGENDADO EM PORTUGUÊS), COMENTANDO SOBRE AS ETAPAS DO CAMINHO.

VÍDEO DE SANDRA (HABLADO EN ESPAÑOL Y CON SUBTÍTULOS EN ESPAÑOL) EN EL QUE COMENTA LAS ETAPAS DEL CAMINO.

LISTEN TO SANDRA (AUDIO IN SPANISH WITH SUBTITLES IN ENGLISH) TALKING ABOUT THE STAGES OF THE CAMINO.

MONIA MARTINELLI

Costuma-se dizer que o Caminho dá o que você precisa e não o que procura.
Foi exatamente o que aconteceu comigo em 2016, quando conheci um grupo de pessoas que me apresentou o peregrino que abriria – em mim – as portas de San Anton.
Aqui tornei-me hospitaleira-voluntária e percebi, por meio das experiências, que servir, simplesmente, preenche meu coração — uma realização que procurei por anos, mas que não encontrei em nenhuma outra atividade.
Quando um peregrino me perguntou por que eu assumia esse papel, respondi sem hesitar: "Estou onde deveria estar." Uma resposta não planejada, vinda do coração, pronunciada ao mesmo tempo que uma lágrima inesperada escorria pelo meu rosto.
Estou em San Anton há quatro anos, e aqui me sinto em casa.
O tempo me ensinou a não me apegar a este lugar. Sou apenas a guardiã temporária de uma dádiva que pertence a todos os peregrinos.

NOTA DO AUTOR: EU E A CLAUDIA OLIVA CONHECEMOS MONIA QUANDO DECIDIMOS PERNOITAR NAS RUÍNAS DE SAN ANTON, EDIFICAÇÃO QUE UM DIA FOI UM HOSPITAL PARA PEREGRINOS. DURANTE O JANTAR, TESTEMUNHAMOS O ANOITECER, QUANDO VELAS FORAM ACESAS, CONFERINDO UM CLIMA AO MESMO TEMPO ACONCHEGANTE E FANTASMAGÓRICO À CONFRATERNIZAÇÃO QUE ACONTECIA ENTRE OS RESTOS DE PAREDE.

Suele decirse que el Camino da lo que uno necesita y no lo que busca.
Eso fue justamente lo que me ocurrió en 2016, cuando conocí a un grupo de personas que me presentaron al peregrino que abriría –en mí– las puertas de San Antón.
Aquí me hice hospitalera voluntaria y me di cuenta, por experiencia propia, que el servir simplemente me llena el corazón. Algo que había buscado durante años, pero que no había encontrado en ninguna actividad.
Cuando un peregrino me preguntó por qué desempeñaba este papel, mi respuesta fue inmediata: "Estoy donde debería estar". Una respuesta que me salió sin pensar, que vino del corazón junto con una lágrima.
Llevo cuatro años aquí y me siento en casa.
El tiempo fue pasando y enseñándome a no apegarme a San Antón. Actualmente, soy la encargada de mantener este lugar que es un regalo para todos los peregrinos.

NOTA DEL AUTOR: CLAUDIA OLIVA Y YO CONOCIMOS A MONIA CUANDO DECIDIMOS PASAR LA NOCHE EN LAS RUINAS DE SAN ANTÓN, LUGAR QUE UN DÍA FUERA HOSPITAL DE PEREGRINOS. DURANTE LA CENA, VIMOS EL ANOCHECER, VELAS QUE SE FUERON ENCENDIENDO Y CREANDO UN AMBIENTE ACOGEDOR Y FANTASMAGÓRICO EN LA CONFRATERNIZACIÓN DE LA QUE PARTICIPÁBAMOS ENTRE LAS PAREDES REMANENTES.

There is a current saying that the Camino gives you what you need, not what you're looking for.
That is exactly what happened to me in 2016, when I met a group of people who introduced me to the pilgrim who would open – within me – the doors of San Anton.
There, I became a volunteer hospitalera[1] and, through my experiences, I realized that serving simply fills my heart. It's the fulfillment I had been looking for all these years and could not find in any other activity.
When a pilgrim asked me why I was a volunteer, I said without hesitation: I'm right where I'm supposed to be! An unplanned answer, coming from the heart, uttered as an unexpected tear fell.
I've been here for four years and this is my home.
Time has passed and taught me not to get attached to San Anton. I am currently the keeper of this place, which is meant to be a gift to all pilgrims.

AUTHOR'S NOTE: CLAUDIA OLIVA AND I MET MONIA WHEN WE DECIDED TO SPEND A NIGHT IN THE RUINS OF SAN ANTON, A PLACE THAT WAS ONCE A HOSPITAL FOR PILGRIMS. DURING DINNER, NIGHT FELL AND CANDLES WERE LIT, CREATING A REASSURING YET SPECTRAL AMBIENCE FOR THE PEOPLE GATHERED IN THE RUINS OF WALLS.

1 - "VOLUNTEER HOSPITALEROS" IS A GROUP FORMED BY FORMER PILGRIMS WHO DECIDED TO, ALTRUISTICALLY AND VOLUNTARILY, TAKE CARE OF/ HOST PILGRIMS IN THE FREE LODGINGS OF THE *CAMINO*

IMAGENS DE SAN ANTON SE ENCONTRAM NAS PÁGINAS 100-101 E 106-107.

SE PUEDEN ENCONTRAR IMÁGENES DE SAN ANTÓN EN PÁGINAS 100-101 Y 106-107.

IMAGES OF SAN ANTON ARE SHOWN IN THE PAGES 100-101 AND 106-107.

TOMÁS MARTINEZ

Minha vida mudou em 1986, durante uma peregrinação. Naquela ocasião, ouvi cantos gregorianos reverberando nas paredes do Castelo dos Templários, em Ponferrada.
Foi ali que compreendi meu chamado.
Decidi transformar uma antiga escola abandonada num refúgio para peregrinos, bem no coração da então inóspita e desassistida região de Manjarín.
Hoje, o Refúgio Manjarín é um espaço visualmente intenso, uma verdadeira memorabilia da minha fé, representada por uma iconografia variada. É também uma maneira de me apresentar àqueles que chegam, seja por curiosidade ou para pernoitar.
No dia em que o Eduardo esteve aqui, durante uma breve conversa, senti uma espécie de revelação e descrevi em detalhes a realidade de uma brasileira — alguém que jamais tinha visto antes. Ela havia escolhido fazer o Caminho por estar enfrentando um turbilhão em sua vida.
Conduzo três orações por dia. Visto meu manto de cavaleiro templário e empunho uma espada. É um ritual de entrega.
Para mim, o Caminho é uma jornada de silêncio e meditação — uma oportunidade rara para me afastar dos ruídos sociais e elevar o nível de consciência.
Acredito que as pessoas devem trabalhar na Terra, para que o Céu lhes conceda tudo o que necessitam.

IMAGEM DE TOMÁS MARTINEZ SE ENCONTRA NAS PÁGINAS 82 E 83.

Mi vida cambió en 1986 cuando, durante una peregrinación, escuché cantos gregorianos resonando en los muros del Castillo de los Templarios en Ponferrada.
En ese momento, comprendí cuál era mi vocación. Decidí convertir una antigua escuela abandonada en un refugio para peregrinos, en pleno corazón de la entonces inhóspita y desatendida localidad de Manjarín.
Hoy en día, el Refugio Manjarín es un espacio visualmente intenso, un verdadero recordatorio de mi fe, representada por una variada iconografía. También es una forma de darme a conocer a las personas que llegan, ya sea por curiosidad o para pasar la noche.
El día que Eduardo estuvo aquí, durante una breve conversación, sentí una especie de revelación y describí con detalle la realidad de una mujer brasileña, alguien a quien nunca había visto antes. Ella había elegido hacer el Camino porque estaba en una etapa bastante turbulenta de su vida.
Rezo tres veces al día. Visto mi manto de caballero templario y empuño una espada. Es un rito de entrega.
Para mí, el Camino es un tiempo de silencio y meditación, una rara oportunidad de alejarse de la convivencia social y elevar el nivel de consciencia.
Creo que las personas deben trabajar en la Tierra para que el Cielo les conceda lo que necesiten.

IMAGEN DE TOMÁS MARTINEZ SE ENCUENTRA EN LAS PÁGINAS 82 Y 83.

My life changed in 1986, during a pilgrimage. On that occasion, I heard Gregorian chants reverberating from the walls of the Templars Castle, in Ponferrada.
There I understood my calling.
I decided to transform an old abandoned school into a refuge for pilgrims, right in the core of what was the inhospitable and unassisted region of Manjarín.
Nowadays, the Manjarín Refuge is a visually intense space, a true memorabilia of my faith, represented by a varied iconography. It is also the way I introduce myself to those who arrive, whether out of curiosity or to stay overnight.
The day Eduardo was here, during a brief conversation, I had a kind of revelation and described in detail what was going on with a Brazilian woman; someone I had never met before. She committed to go through the Camino because she was facing a turmoil in her life.
I perform three prayers a day. I wear my Knight Templar cloak and wield a sword. It is a ritual of surrender.
For me, the Camino is a journey of silence and meditation; a rare opportunity to set aside the social noise and raise the level of consciousness.
I believe that people should work on Earth, so that Heaven can provide what they need.

IMAGE OF TOMÁS MARTINEZ IS SHOWN IN THE PAGES 82 AND 83.

CHUN-SHEN SAM, CHEN

Em El Acebo de San Miguel conheci o Eduardo, enquanto eu preparava minha bicicleta para seguir viagem. Tinha começado meu trajeto em Pamplona e seguia rumo a Santiago.
Este sou eu: Chun-Shen Sam, professor titular de matemática aposentado, de Taiwan.
Aos 78 anos, decidi pedalar sozinho, movido pelo desafio e pelo desejo de percorrer esses 700 km.
Minha esposa é budista, meus filhos são cristãos. Para mim, Deus se manifesta na natureza, e o Caminho é uma forma de estar mais próximo Dele.
Com minha família, combinei algo simples e objetivo: se eu não desse sinal de vida em 48 horas, enviariam o resgate.
No reencontro com Eduardo em Samos, demos boas risadas enquanto eu tentava aprender algumas palavras em espanhol. "¡Jugo de naranja!", eu repetia, rindo do meu sotaque.
Na última vez em que nos vimos, no Cebreiro, contei que havia dormido ao relento na noite anterior. Me perdi na dura subida até o vilarejo celta e, quando cheguei, tudo já estava fechado.
Mas estava preparado: usei meu saco de dormir, vesti o casaco e nada de grave me aconteceu.
Dividi esse relato logo cedo, por volta das seis da manhã, antes mesmo do meu café. E posso garantir: nem o frio, nem o contratempo foram capazes de tirar meu bom humor.
Continuo animado — sou movido por uma fé silenciosa e pela inspiração de cada novo dia no Caminho.

Conocí a Eduardo en El Acebo de San Miguel mientras preparaba mi bicicleta para continuar el viaje que había comenzado en Pamplona rumbo a Santiago.
Soy Chun-Shen Sam, profesor titular de matemáticas jubilado de Taiwán. A los 78 años decidí pedalear solo, motivado por el reto y el deseo de recorrer estos 700 km.
Mi mujer es budista, mis hijos son cristianos. Para mí, Dios se manifiesta en la naturaleza y el Camino es una forma de estar más cerca de Él.
Tengo un trato simple y objetivo con mi familia: si no doy señales de vida en 48 horas, ellos se ponen en contacto con el servicio de rescate.
Cuando volví a encontrarme a Eduardo en Samos, nos reímos mucho de mis intentos de aprender algunas palabras en español. "¡Zumo de naranja!", repetía riéndome de mi acento.
La última vez que nos vimos, en O Cebreiro, le conté que la noche anterior había dormido al raso. Me perdí en la dura subida al poblado celta y, cuando llegué, estaba todo cerrado.
Pero estaba preparado: me abrigué, me metí en el saco de dormir y no pasó nada.
Era muy pronto cuando se lo conté, las seis de la mañana, antes de desayunar. Lo que puedo asegurar es que ni el frío ni ese contratiempo fueron capaces de empañar mi buen humor.
Continúo animado, una fe silenciosa y la inspiración de cada nuevo día en el Camino es lo que me motiva.

I first met Chun-Shen Sam in El Acebo de San Miguel as he prepared his bicycle to continue the journey that had begun in Pamplona and would end in Santiago.
This retired professor of mathematics from Taiwan was cycling alone, motivated by the challenge of covering 700 km at the age of 78.
His wife was a Buddhist, and his children were Christians. For him, the representation of God on Earth is nature, and the *Camino* the path to get closer to Him.
He said he had an agreement with his family: no signs of life within 48 hours, and they would send a rescue team.
The focus of the conversation at our next meeting in Samos was his effort to learn, with a lot of laughter, a few words of Spanish – Jugo de Naranja!
The last time we met, in Cebreiro, he said he had slept outside that night, as he had got lost on the difficult climb to the Celtic village. When he eventually arrived, everything had already been closed. Protected from the cold by a sleeping bag and jacket, he said that nothing serious had happened to him.
I heard this story at around six in the morning, before he had had any coffee. Yet, nothing seemed to dampen the good humor and spirit of this man, one of my inspirations on the *Camino*.

JESÚS JATO

No meu albergue Ave Fénix, preparo a Queimada do Orujo[1] com aguardentes de todos os tipos.
Faço isso devagar, com alma, com humor, de forma espirituosa.
Antes do ritual, sempre aviso: "Não cheguem muito perto, pois vocês podem se queimar." E, então, emendo em galego, invocando os elementos, começando por Santiago, Senhor dos Quatro Ventos.
E prossigo:

"Pombos, corujas, sapos e bruxas...
Peregrinos que andam buscando o engano, buscando refúgio com sauna, piscina e banho.
Peregrinos com carros de apoio, em pontos de ônibus ou de taxi.
Peregrinos com tendinites, 'bolhites' e 'preguicites'.
Peregrinos madrugadores e roncadores.
Com este fogo, levantarei chamas que iluminarão o inferno, obrigando as bruxas a descer de suas vassouras e a tomar banho na praia da sardinha gorda.
Vamos invocar novamente...as Forças do Ar, Terra, Mar e Fogo.
E quando esta mistura descer pela nossa garganta, estaremos livres de todos os maus espíritos e feitiços.
E que todo este momento de união mística purifique o ambiente e o Caminho seja de paz, luz e amor.
Podem acender as luzes."

NOTA DO AUTOR: UM MISTO DE HOSPITALEIRO, MÉDICO, COZINHEIRO, FILÓSOFO E *SHOWMAN* – JESÚS DEIXA MARCAS DE SIMPLICIDADE E GENEROSIDADE EM QUEM DESFRUTA UM POUCO DA SUA COMPANHIA E MAGIA. [1] BEBIDA ORIGINÁRIA DA GALÍCIA, DEDICADA AO DESCONHECIDO E, DE ALGUM MODO, MÁGICO. DURANTE SUA PREPARAÇÃO SE FAZ UM CONJURO NO QUAL SÃO INVOCADOS OS QUATRO ELEMENTOS (FOGO, TERRA, ÁGUA E AR).

ÁUDIO ORIGINAL DE JESÚS JATO (EM ESPANHOL E GALEGO) FAZENDO A QUEIMADA DO ORUJO.

En mi albergue Ave Fénix, preparo la Queimada de Orujo[1] con aguardientes de todo tipo. Es algo que hago despacio, con alma, buen humor y emoción.
Antes del ritual, siempre aviso: "No os acerquéis mucho que os podéis quemar".
Inmediatamente después, paso a invocar en gallego los elementos, comenzando por Santiago, Señor de los Cuatro Vientos. Y sigo: "Palomas, lechuzas, sapos y brujas...
Peregrinos que andan buscando el engaño, buscando refugio con sauna, piscina y baño.
Peregrinos con coche de apoyo, en paradas de autobús o de taxi.
Peregrinos con tendinitis, 'ampollitis' y 'vaguitis'.
Peregrinos madrugadores y roncadores. Con este fuego levantaré llamas que alumbren el infierno, para forzar a las brujas a bajar de sus escobas y bañarse en la playa de la sardina gorda. Vamos a invocar otra vez... las Fuerzas del Aire, de la Tierra, del Mar y del Fuego.
Y cuando esta mezcla deslice por nuestras gargantas, quedaremos libres de todos los malos espíritus y hechizos.
Que este momento de unión mística purifique el ambiente y que el Camino sea de paz, luz y amor.
Podéis encender las luces".

NOTA DEL AUTOR: MEZCLA DE HOSPITALERO, MÉDICO, COCINERO, FILÓSOFO Y *SHOWMAN*, JESÚS DEJA UNA HUELLA DE SENCILLEZ Y GENEROSIDAD EN QUIEN DISFRUTA UN POCO DE SU COMPAÑÍA Y MAGIA.
1- BEBIDA ORIGINARIA DE GALICIA, RELACIONADA CON TODO AQUELLO QUE NO CONOCEMOS Y DE ALGÚN MODO MÁGICO, EN CUYA PREPARACIÓN SE HACE UN CONJURO EN EL QUE SE CITAN LOS CUATRO ELEMENTOS (FUEGO, TIERRA, AGUA Y AIRE).

AUDIO ORIGINAL DE JESÚS JATO (EN ESPAÑOL Y GALLEGO) MIENTRAS PREPARA LA QUEIMADA DE ORUJO.

At my Ave Fénix hostel, I prepare Queimada do Orujo[1] with spirits of all types. I do it slowly, with soul and humor, in a witty way.
I always warn people before the ritual: 'Don't get too close, as you could get burned'. Then, in Galician, invoking the elements starting with Santiago, Lord of the Four Winds, I pronounce:
'Pigeons, owls, frogs and witches...
Pilgrims who are seeking the deceit, seeking refuge with a sauna, swimming pool and bath.
Pilgrims with support vehicles, at bus or taxi stops.
Pilgrims with tendonitis, 'blisteritis' and 'sluggishnessitis'.
Early risers and snorers' pilgrims.
With this fire, I will raise flames that will illuminate hell, forcing witches to get off their brooms and take a bath on the beach of the fat sardine.
Let's invoke again... the Forces of Air, Earth, Sea and Fire.
And when this drink goes down our throat, we will be free from all evil spirits and spells.
May this entire moment of mystical union purify the environment and the *Camino* be one of peace, light and love.
You can turn on the lights.'

AUTHOR'S NOTE: A MIX OF HOST, DOCTOR, COOK, PHILOSOPHER AND SHOWMAN – JESÚS LEAVES A MARK OF SIMPLICITY AND GENEROSITY ON THOSE WHO ENJOY HIS COMPANY AND MAGIC.
1- A DRINK ORIGINARY FROM GALICIA, OFFERED TO THE UNKNOWN AND, SOMEHOW, MAGIC. DURING ITS PREPARATION, A CONJURE IS MADE IN WHICH THE FOUR ELEMENTS (FIRE, EARTH, WATER AND AIR) ARE INVOKED.

LISTEN TO JESÚS JATO SPEAKING (IN SPANISH AND GALICIAN) WHILE HE PERFORMS THE QUEIMADA DO ORUJO.

ANNETTE DÖLLE

Comecei o Caminho em Saint-Jean-Pied-de-Port, na França, no dia 16 de julho de 2017, e peregrinei até Santiago por trinta e dois dias, incluindo dois de descanso.
Nesta minha segunda peregrinação, fui de um momento ao outro sem perceber, sem planejar, como as águas de um rio deslizando em sua correnteza, contornando obstáculos e abrindo caminhos.
Fiquei cansada, tive bolhas, os músculos doeram, no entanto, prosseguir sempre foi o único sentido. Não havia outra possibilidade.
Essa insistente, contínua e ritmada movimentação me transporta a um estado emocional permeável a pensamentos, insights, memórias e músicas. Às vezes, preciso apenas cantar uma música. Tenho muitas em meu repertório.
No fim do dia, quando cessa a jornada, sinto a necessidade de refletir e processar tudo o que emergiu dessa meditação ativa. Escrever é útil, não só para concretizar as ideias, mas também como faxina mental, que me revigora para o dia seguinte.
Esse ritual se repetiu diariamente ao longo de um mês, favorecendo uma transformação gradual no estado de espírito, o acesso a campos mais sutis e o desenvolvimento da atenção plena.

Comencé el Camino en Saint-Jean-Pied-de-Port, Francia, el 16 de julio de 2017, y peregriné hasta Santiago durante treinta y dos días, dos de ellos de descanso.
En esta segunda peregrinación, fui de un momento a otro sin darme cuenta, sin planearlo, como el agua que sigue la corriente del río, sorteando obstáculos y abriendo camino.
Me cansé, tuve ampollas, me dolían los músculos, pero avanzar era siempre lo único que tenía sentido, no había alternativa.
Este movimiento insistente, continuo y rítmico me transporta a un estado emocional permeable a pensamientos, percepciones, recuerdos y canciones. A veces lo único que tengo que hacer es cantar una canción. Tengo muchas en mi repertorio.
Al final del día, cuando termina la jornada, uno necesita reflexionar y procesar el material de esta meditación activa. Escribir es útil, no solo para plasmar las ideas, sino también para limpiar la mente y recuperarse para el día siguiente.
Este ritual se realiza diariamente a lo largo de un mes, transformando poco a poco el estado de ánimo, entrando en contacto con campos más sutiles y desarrollando la atención plena.

I started the *Camino* in Saint-Jean-Pied-de-Port, in France, on July 16, 2017, and it took me 32 days to reach Santiago, including two days set aside to rest.
This time, on my second pilgrimage, I went from one moment to the next without realizing it, without planning it, like the waters of a river drifting with the current, bypassing obstacles and opening new channels.
I was tired, I had blisters, my muscles ached, but carrying on was always the only way forward, there was no other possibility.
This persistent, continuous, and rhythmic movement takes me to an emotional state permeable to thoughts, insights, memories, and music. Sometimes, I just need to sing a song. I have many in my repertoire.
At the end of the day, when we pause our journey, it is necessary to reflect and process the material from this active meditation. Writing is useful, not only to put down ideas, but also to cleanse the mind, to strengthen oneself for the next day.
This ritual was repeated daily over the course of a month, allowing a gradual change in my state of mind, the contact with more subtle matters, and the development of mindfulness.

VÍDEO (FALADO EM INGLÊS E LEGENDADO EM PORTUGUÊS) DA ANNETTE, FALANDO DA PEREGRINAÇÃO COMO FORMA DE MEDITAÇÃO ATIVA E CANTANDO UMA MÚSICA.

VÍDEO (EN INGLÉS CON SUBTÍTULOS EN ESPAÑOL) DE ANNETTE EN EL QUE HABLA DE LA PEREGRINACIÓN COMO FORMA DE MEDITACIÓN ACTIVA Y CANTA UNA CANCIÓN.

LISTEN TO ANNETTE (IN ENGLISH, WITH SUBTITLES IN ENGLISH) SPEAKING ABOUT THE PILGRIMAGE AS A METHOD OF ACTIVE MEDITATION AND SINGING A SONG.

AGRADECIMENTOS

Nenhum caminho se percorre sozinho. Este livro nasceu do passo firme, mas também do olhar generoso, das mãos estendidas ao longo da trilha até aqui.

Agradeço à Luciana Chehin, minha companheira e esposa, pelo apoio, torcida, paciência, bom humor, opiniões, pela parceria. Sua colaboração foi essencial para o sucesso desta empreitada. Valeu a pena o esforço concentrado ao longo de vários anos.

Reconheço e honro o apoio da minha família antes e durante o processo de realização desta obra. Sem essa base sólida, não teria alcançado este resultado, do qual tanto me orgulho.

A realização deste projeto se estendeu no tempo, portanto, a lista de agradecimentos é extensa.
Sem a participação destas pessoas, este livro não seria o que é. São elas: Acácio Luiz Costa, Akira Goto, Alfredo Reickdal, Ana Silvia Forgiarini (Frida Projetos Culturais), Antonio Pastore, Celio Coscia, Cibele Rodrigues, Cris Duarte, Diana Risso- Gill, Djalma Dutra (Ciclo Caravelle), Gabriel Martinez (in memoriam), Ignacio Aronovich, Javier Lopez del Pino, Malila Ohki, João Carlos Brasil, João Paulo Barbosa, João Paulo Lorenzon, Julio Menezes, Leilson Caixeta, Lucas de Sena Lima, Marcia de Mitri, Marcos Felix, Maribel (Albergue La Cachava, em Castrojeriz), Maurizio Mancioli, Monia Martinelli, Pamella Melo, Paola Schmid, Rafael Campos, Regiane Santos Basan, Renato Ciasca, Rita Sastre, Vanderson Afonso e Walkiria Dutra.

Aulus Sellmer foi quem me colocou no projeto "Desafios pelo Mundo", realizado por ele e pelo então diretor executivo Acácio Luiz Costa das rádios *Eldorado* e *Estadão*. Foi para eles que eu captei as primeiras imagens que iriam, quase dez anos depois, originar este livro. A eles, meu muito obrigado, pela confiança e parceria de longa data.

Agradeço à Claudia Oliva, minha namorada à época e companheira da segunda viagem. Sem ela, esta obra não existiria, já que foi dela a ideia de perpetuar as imagens em uma publicação.

Honro a contribuição e incentivo do meu irmão, João Henrique Calderan Quintino, com quem tive inúmeras conversas sobre fotografia, vida e arte em geral. Ele, que foi fotógrafo por muitos anos, acompanhou este percurso desde o início e trouxe reflexões sempre pertinentes.

A produtora cultural Sofia Fan foi uma das primeiras pessoas a conhecer este projeto e logo fomentou sua execução, me apresentando os fotógrafos Iatã Cannabrava e André Penteado. O Iatã me introduziu ao universo do fotolivro, que me revelou conceitos que eu desconhecia.
O André foi um agente transformador do meu olhar. Através da nossa troca e por acompanhar seus grupos de estudo, fui compreendendo a fotografia conceitual em contraponto à documental e jornalística, meu berço estético.

A fotógrafa Mayra Erlich entrou "no time" por sugestão do André Penteado. Sua participação, como editora de imagens, na construção da narrativa visual, foi crucial para a guinada conceitual desta edição.

O fotógrafo Roberto Setton, que muito positivamente contribuiu com este livro, me apresentou ao diretor de arte Ciro Girard, com o qual me conectei de imediato. Desenvolver o projeto gráfico e a editoração com o Ciro foi bem prazeroso. Na verdade, o seu envolvimento foi além da parte visual-estrutural. Com sua experiência e generosidade, Ciro engrandeceu demais o resultado final. Meu agradecimento a ambos.

Após a Luciana Chehin, o engenheiro e poeta Paulo Ludmer, a quem sou bastante grato, foi o primeiro a ler meus textos e, com espírito crítico, agregou sabedoria e poesia a eles. É dele também a grande maioria dos títulos das imagens, para as quais adicionou camadas de entendimento e pontos de vista originais.

O processo de confecção das versões de meus textos em espanhol (Nuria Mauleón Montes e Juan Blanco) e inglês (Mirjam & Jeff Moylan, e Magali Gallello), assim como a revisão em português (Paulo Ludmer, Magali Gallello e Sergio Tulio Caldas) foi precioso.

Acompanhar o enriquecimento em português e a transformação para que estas peças pudessem ser compreendidas em outras línguas foi curioso, interessante, mágico. A estes profissionais meu muito obrigado pela dedicação e empenho.
Aprendi muito com vocês.

AGRADECIMIENTOS

Ningún camino se hace a solas. Este libro nació no solo de pasos firmes, sino también de miradas generosas y manos tendidas a lo largo de la ruta recorrida hasta aquí.

Quiero agradecer a Luciana Chehin, mi compañera y esposa, por su apoyo, entusiasmo, paciencia, buen humor, opiniones y complicidad. Su colaboración fue esencial para el éxito de esta aventura.

Reconozco y valoro el apoyo de mi familia antes y durante el proceso de realización de esta obra. Sin esta base sólida, no habría alcanzado este resultado, del cual me siento muy orgulloso.

La realización de este proyecto se extendió, por lo que la lista de agradecimientos fue aumentando. Sin la participación de estas personas, que cito a continuación, el resultado de este libro no sería el mismo: Acácio Luiz Costa, Akira Goto, Alfredo Reickdal, Ana Silvia Forgiarini (Frida Projetos Culturais), Antonio Pastore, Celio Coscia, Cibele Rodrigues, Cris Duarte, Diana Risso-Gill, Djalma Dutra (Ciclo Caravelle), Gabriel Martínez (*in memoriam*), Ignacio Aronovich, Javier López del Pino, Malila Ohki, João Carlos Brasil, João Paulo Barbosa, João Paulo Lorenzon, Julio Menezes, Leilson Caixeta, Lucas de Sena Lima, Marcia de Mitri, Marcos Felix, Maribel (Albergue La Cachava en Castrojeriz), Maurizio Mancioli, Monia Martinelli, Pamella Melo, Paola Schmid, Rafael Campos, Regiane Santos Basan, Renato Ciasca, Rita Sastre, Vanderson Afonso y Walkiria Dutra.

Aulus Sellmer me implicó en el proyecto Desafíos por el Mundo, realizado por él y por Acácio Luiz Costa, en aquella época director ejecutivo de las radios Eldorado y Estadão. Fue para ellos para quienes capté las primeras imágenes que, casi diez años después, darían lugar a este libro. Muchas gracias a ambos por su confianza y colaboración de tanto tiempo.

Quiero agradecer a Claudia Oliva, mi novia en aquella época y compañera en el segundo viaje. Sin ella, este trabajo no hubiese sido posible, ya que partió de ella la idea de perpetuar las imágenes en una publicación.

Quiero dedicar un especial reconocimiento a mi hermano, João Henrique Calderan Quintino, por sus innumerables conversaciones sobre fotografía, vida y arte en general que tanto estimularon y contribuyeron a este proyecto. Él, que fue fotógrafo durante muchos años, siguió el proceso desde el principio y señaló cuestiones siempre pertinentes.

La productora cultural Sofia Fan fue una de las primeras personas que conoció este proyecto y enseguida fomentó su realización, presentándome a los fotógrafos Iatã Cannabrava y André Penteado. Iatã me introdujo en el mundo de los fotolibros, lo que me reveló conceptos que no conocía. André fue un agente de transformación de mi perspectiva. A través de nuestros intercambios y siguiendo sus grupos de estudio, fui entendiendo la fotografía conceptual en contraposición a la fotografía documental y periodística, mi cuna estética.

La fotógrafa Mayra Erlich se incorporó al "equipo" por sugerencia de André Penteado. Su participación, como editora de imágenes, en el desarrollo de la narrativa visual fue crucial para el giro conceptual de esta edición.

El fotógrafo Roberto Setton, que contribuyó muy positivamente a este libro, me presentó al director de arte Ciro Girard, con quien conecté inmediatamente. Desarrollar el diseño gráfico y la edición con Ciro fue un auténtico placer. En realidad, su implicación fue más allá de la parte estructural y visual. Con su experiencia y generosidad, Ciro realmente le dio otra magnitud al resultado final. Mi agradecimiento a ambos.

Después de Luciana Chehin, el ingeniero y poeta Paulo Ludmer, a quien estoy muy agradecido, fue quien primero leyó mis textos y, con espíritu crítico, les añadió sabiduría y poesía. También son suyos la gran mayoría de los títulos de las imágenes, a las que sumó comprensión y un original punto de vista.

El proceso de elaboración de las versiones de mis textos en español (Nuria Mauleón Montes y Juan Blanco) e inglés (Mirjam & Jeff Moylan y Magali Gallello), así como la revisión en portugués (Paulo Ludmer, Magali Gallello y Sergio Tulio Caldas) fue primoroso. Seguir de cerca el enriquecimiento en portugués y la transformación para que estas piezas pudieran entenderse en otros idiomas fue curioso, interesante, mágico. Agradezco a estos profesionales su dedicación y compromiso. He aprendido mucho con todos vosotros.

ACKNOWLEDGEMENTS

There is no path taken alone. This book came out of the steadfast step, but also from the generous look and helping hands along the way until here.

I would like to thank Luciana Chehin, my partner and wife, for her support, patience, good humor, understanding, opinion, well, for her complicity. Her collaboration was essential to the success of this endeavor.

I value and honor my family, for the support throughout the creation and development of this work and beyond as well. Without a solid foundation, I would not have achieved this result, of which I am very proud.

This project has been a long time coming, so the list of acknowledgements kept growing. Without the engagement of the people named below the result of this book would not be the same: Akira Goto, Alfredo Reickdal, Ana Silvia Forgiarini (Frida Projetos Culturais), Antonio Pastore, Celio Coscia, Cibele Rodrigues, Cris Duarte, Diana Risso-Gill, Djalma Dutra (Ciclo Caravelle), Gabriel Martínez (*in memoriam*), Ignacio Aronovich, Javier López del Pino, Malila Ohki, João Carlos Brasil, João Paulo Barbosa, João Paulo Lorenzon, Julio Menezes, Leilson Caixeta, Lucas de Sena Lima, Marcia de Mitri, Marcos Felix, Maribel (Albergue La Cachava in Castrojeriz), Maurizio Mancioli, Monia Martinelli, Pamella Melo, Paola Schmid, Rafael Campos, Regiane Santos Basan, Renato Ciasca, Rita Sastre, Vanderson Afonso and Walkiria Dutra.

Aulus Sellmer was the one who got me involved in the "Desafios pelo Mundo" project, a production devised by him and then commercial director Acácio Luiz Costa for the Eldorado and Estadão radio stations. It was for them that I captured the first images which, almost ten years later, were to give rise to this book. Many thanks to Acácio for believing in my work, and to Aulus for his trust and partnership over many years.

I want to thank Claudia Oliva, my girlfriend at the time and my partner on the second trip. Without her, this work would not have been possible, since it was her idea to perpetuate the images in a publication.

I would like to dedicate a special acknowledgement to my brother, João Henrique Calderan Quintino, for our countless conversations about photography, life and art in general. He, who was a photographer for many years, followed the progress from the very beginning, pointing aspects that were always pertinent.

Cultural producer Sofia Fan was one of the first persons to learn about this project and soon encouraged its implementation, putting me in contact with photographers Iatã Cannabrava and André Penteado. Iatã introduced me to the world of photobooks, which revealed concepts I had not come across before. André changed my perspective at looking at things. Through our exchanges and following his study groups, I came to understand conceptual photography as opposed to documentary and journalistic photography, my original cradle of aesthetics.

I am grateful to photographer Mayra Erlich, who joined the team at the suggestion of André Penteado. Her participation, as image editor, in the construction of the visual narrative, was crucial for the conceptual definition of this book.

Photographer Roberto Setton, who contributed so much to this book, introduced me to art director Ciro Girard, with whom I immediately connected. Developing the graphic design and editorial work with Ciro was a real pleasure. In fact, his involvement went beyond the visual-structural part. With his experience and generosity, Ciro truly enhanced the final result. My thanks to both of them.

After Luciana Chehin, Paulo Ludmer, engineer and poet, to whom I am very grateful, was the first to read my texts and, with a critical spirit, added wisdom and poetry to them. The vast majority of the image captions, to which he added layers of understanding and original points of view, are also his.

The review of the Portuguese version (Paulo Ludmer, Magali Gallello and Sergio Tulio Caldas) as well as the translation into Spanish (Nuria Mauleón Montes and Juan Blanco) and English (Mirjam & Jeff Moylan and Magali Gallello) turned into a precious experience. Watching how the Portuguese language was enriched, how the source texts transformed so that they could be understood in other languages, was curious, interesting and magical. Many thanks to these professionals for their dedication and commitment. I have learned a lot from you.

O AUTOR E SEU CAMINHO

EL AUTOR Y SU CAMINO / ABOUT THE AUTHOR

Eduardo Calderan Quintino nasceu em Curitiba, em 02 de janeiro de 1966. Aos sete anos, mudou-se com a família para São Paulo e, ainda menino, a pé ou de bicicleta, descobriu-se um explorador urbano. Apaixonado por desbravar o novo — herança do pai, Annário Rocha Quintino — e movido por curiosidade pelas histórias dos outros — legado da mãe, Therezinha Calderan Quintino —, assim se integrou ao mundo.
Durante o curso de Rádio e Televisão na FAAP (Fundação Armando Alvares Penteado, São Paulo), assistiu uma palestra sobre a chegada da MTV no Brasil e percebeu que faria parte daquele universo. Por quatro anos, integrou como cinegrafista a equipe que iniciou a emissora. Atuando como documentarista envolveu--se com as Corridas de Aventura, em parceria com o amigo cineasta Renato Ciasca, experiência que lhe permitiu dominar diversas ferramentas profissionais.
Nesse contexto conheceu o preparador físico Aulus Sellmer, que o convidou para registrar sua peregrinação, pontapé inicial deste livro.
O hábito da prática da meditação encontrou ressonância no Caminho de Santiago de Compostela, assim como a percepção da força integradora da natureza na construção do silêncio interno, um estado sempre almejado em peregrinação.
Desse balaio, nasceu este livro.

Eduardo Calderan Quintino nació en Curitiba el 2 de enero de 1966. A los siete años se mudó con su familia a São Paulo y, desde pequeño, a pie o en bicicleta, se descubrió a sí mismo como explorador urbano. Su pasión por conocer lo nuevo, heredada de su padre, y la curiosidad por la historia de los demás, que le vino de su madre, le facilitaron su integración en el mundo.
Mientras cursaba sus estudios de Radio y Televisión en FAAP (Fundação Armando Alvares Penteado, São Paulo), tuvo la ocasión de acudir a una conferencia sobre la llegada de MTV a Brasil y, en ese momento, se dio cuenta de que formaría parte de aquel mundo. Durante cuatro años, fue cámara del equipo que puso en marcha la emisora. Empezó a participar como documentalista en carreras de aventura en colaboración con su amigo cineasta Renato Ciasca, lo que le permitió dominar diferentes herramientas profesionales.
Luego conoció al preparador físico Aulus Sellmer, quien le invitó a documentar su peregrinaje, lo que dio pie a este libro.
El hábito de meditar encajó con el Camino de Santiago, así como la percepción del poder integrador de la naturaleza en la construcción del silencio interior, algo siempre deseado en las peregrinaciones.
Con esos mimbres, se urdió este libro.

Eduardo Calderan Quintino was born in Curitiba on January 2, 1966. At the age of seven, the family moved to São Paulo, where, as a young boy, on foot or by bike, he became an urban explorer. Passionate about *exploring the unknown*, a trait inherited from his father, and *curious about the history of others*, his mother's legacy, he found his place in the world.
While studying Radio and Television at FAAP (Fundação Armando Alvares Penteado, São Paulo), he attended a lecture on the arrival of MTV in Brazil and realized that he wanted to be part of that universe. For four years, he was a cameraman on the team that started the network. As a documentary filmmaker, he became involved in Corridas de Aventura (Trail Runs), in partnership with his filmmaker friend Renato Ciasca. In due course, he became proficient in a number of professional tools.
Then he met fitness trainer Aulus Sellmer, who invited him to document the latter's pilgrimage, the starting point for this book.
His habit of practicing meditation fitted in with the essence of the *Camino de Santiago de Compostela*, as did the insight of how much nature contributes to build internal silence, something always to seek on pilgrimages.
From this background, this book was born.

Nota de Reconhecimento e Respeito à Imagem
Foram feitos todos os esforços para identificar e contatar as pessoas retratadas nesta publicação, respeitando seu direito de imagem e privacidade. Caso alguém não tenha sido localizado, estamos à disposição para eventuais correções em futuras edições. Esta obra foi feita com profundo respeito por todos os retratados.
Para qualquer esclarecimento, entre em contato:
eduardo.quintino@gmail.com

Nota de Reconocimiento y Respeto a la Imagen
Se han hecho todos los esfuerzos posibles para identificar y contactar a las personas retratadas en esta publicación, respetando su derecho de imagen y privacidad. Si alguna persona no fue localizada por error, quedamos a disposición para realizar correcciones en futuras ediciones.
Esta obra fue realizada con profundo respeto por todos los retratados.
Para cualquier consulta, escriba a:
eduardo.quintino@gmail.com

Image Rights and Acknowledgment Notice
Every effort has been made to identify and contact the individuals portrayed in this publication, respecting their right to image and privacy. If someone was unintentionally not reached, we remain available to make corrections in future editions. This work was created with deep respect for all those depicted.
For any inquiries, please contact:
eduardo.quintino@gmail.com

Contato
celular +5511 99942-7360
email eduardo.quintino@gmail.com
instagram @quintinoeduardocalderan

FICHA TÉCNICA

Imagens e textos
Imágenes y textos / Images and texts
EDUARDO CALDERAN QUINTINO

Edição de imagens
Edición de las imágenes / Image editing
MAÍRA ERLICH E EDUARDO QUINTINO

Projeto gráfico e editoração
Diseño gráfico y edicion / Graphic design and editing
CIRO GIRARD

Coordenação editorial
Coordinación editorial / Publishing coordination
EDUARDO CALDERAN QUINTINO

Tratamento de imagem
Tratamiento de las imágenes / Image processing
MAÍRA ERLICH E GICLÊ FINE ART

Edição e revisão de texto
Revisión de texto / Proofreading
PAULO LUDMER, MAGALI GALLELLO E SERGIO TULIO CALDAS

Versão em inglês
Traducción al inglés / English version
MIRJAM & JEFF MOYLAN E MAGALI GALLELLO

Versão em espanhol
Traducción al español / Spanish version
NURIA MAULEÓN MONTES E JUAN BLANCO

Ilustração da concha
Ilustración de la concha del peregrino / Shell illustration
CLAUDIA OLIVA

Vídeos e áudios dos QR Codes
Vídeos y audios de los códigos QR / QR code videos and audios
EDUARDO CALDERAN QUINTINO

Transcrição de áudio Jesús Jato
Transcripción del audio Jesús Jato / Audio transcription Jesús Jato
JAVIER LÓPEZ DEL PINO

Produção gráfica
Productor gráfico / Graphic production
HELOISA VASCONCELLOS

Impressão
Impresión / Printing
GRÁFICA IPSIS

Dados Internacionais de Catalogação na Publicação (CIP)
(Câmara Brasileira do Livro, SP, Brasil)

Quintino, Eduardo Calderan
The way = Camino = Caminho / Eduardo Calderan Quintino. -- Cotia, SP : Ed. do Autor, 2025.

ISBN 978-65-01-64382-3

1. Catolicismo 2. Fotografias 3. Peregrinos e peregrinações - Santiago de Compostela 4. Santiago de Compostela - Descrição e viagens 5. Turismo de bicicleta I. Título. II. Título: Camino. III. Título: Caminho.

25-294367.0 CDD-778.9

Índices para catálogo sistemático:

1. Santiago de Compostela : Peregrinos e peregrinações : Registro fotográfico 778.9